T0268255

STRESS LESS

HOW TO ACHIEVE BALANCE AND HARMONY IN YOUR LIFE!

The R.E.A.L. Stress Management Strategy

SAMANTHA CAMPBELL, LCSW, MSW, RSW

ISBN 979-8-98977-550-7
eBook ISBN 979-8-98977-551-4

DEDICATION

To God, whose guidance and grace have empowered me to help others connect with Him and find joy amid life's challenges.

To my husband, for your unwavering support and encouragement at every step.

To my daughter, whose enthusiasm and love have been a constant source of motivation.

To my mother, whose steadfast faith and prayers have inspired me throughout this journey.

To my family, friends, mentors, and church family, for your wisdom, love, and consistent encouragement. Your support has been an incredible blessing, and I am deeply grateful.

TABLE OF CONTENTS

INTRODUCTION

WE LIVE WITH STRESS EVERY DAY. DEALING WITH STRESSFUL situations is just a natural part of the life cycle. Stress is how our bodies respond to any type of pressure in our lives, including deadlines, getting married, competition, graduation, car accidents, and so on. However, researchers have discovered that exposure to stressful situations for long periods can have a negative effect on us. Exposure to stress for long periods can cause us to develop chronic stress symptoms, which can result in serious illnesses and sometimes death. Surprised? I know I was surprised a couple of years ago when I had a health scare that opened my eyes to how chronic stress, if unmanaged, can have a negative impact on your quality of life. I had no idea what chronic stress was or its symptoms, and I was blindsided when it impacted me. I remember struggling with depression and having swollen lymph nodes on the back of my neck; however, I had no clue that the root cause was chronic stress.

I know you are probably wondering what chronic stress has to do with depression and swollen lymph nodes. You will be so amazed to learn about how chronic stress affects our emotions, thoughts, and bodies and how we expose ourselves to situations and environments that are slowly and silently killing us.

I had to seriously reflect on the decisions I was making in my life and how they were impacting my health. After my eyes were opened to my symptoms and what was causing them, I embarked on a journey to reduce my chronic stress symptoms. I started praying, and with the help of God, I made some heart-leaping changes in my life that resulted in my lymph nodes reducing and my depression symptoms drastically minimized!

Curious about how I did it? God revealed to me that I was living unhealthily, and He gave me the strength to make some R.E.A.L. changes in my life. I remember sitting at my kitchen table in spring 2022, reflecting on how I got to a place of feeling healthy and happy. I heard God clearly say to me that I needed to share what I have discovered with others. I was listening to Him; however, instantly, self-doubt showed up. I doubted my ability to do what He was asking of me. Why would people listen to me? How would I do this? What would I say? I took a deep breath and decided to trust God. I love seeing people happy and living their best lives, so if I can help people be around their families longer—live instead of just existing, have good health, and stay out of hospitals—I would nervously follow His lead. I said to myself, "Get it together, Samantha! It's not about you and your vulnerabilities; it's really about what God can do through you!" I took a very long, deep breath to calm my anxiety and asked God to show me how to share this information with people in a way that they would pay attention and actually make changes in their lives. I took up my phone, began typing what the Lord placed on my heart, and wrote "R.E.A.L." Are we really living, or are we just existing? Are we being real with ourselves when we don't take care of our health or when we stay in situations or environments that make us unhappy? Do we really want to know the truth to make the necessary changes in our lives? When I finished typing, the R.E.A.L. Stress Management Strategy was born. I know you are wondering what is the meaning of R.E.A.L.

R. Recognize your symptoms.

E. Educate yourself about how to manage your symptoms.

A. Adjust your life to create the life you need.

L. Live. Love. Laugh.

The R.E.A.L. Stress Management Strategy provides a comprehensive approach to stress management that includes increasing awareness, effective stress management skills to reduce your stress, and life-changing strategies to help you make the changes you need to keep your stress levels low and improve your overall health. It also teaches you how to maintain progress and live a happy, fulfilling life. You will find everything you need in this book to help you prevent and manage chronic stress.

This strategy summarizes my journey to better physical, emotional, and spiritual health, and I can't wait to share it with you.

CHAPTER 1

PART 1 - HOW STRESS IMPACTS OUR BODIES

Worry and stress affect the circulation, the heart, the glands, and the whole nervous system, and profoundly affect heart action.

– Charles W. Mayo, M.D.

I MOVED FROM JAMAICA TO CANADA WHEN I WAS TWEN-ty-seven years old. I was excited to live in a new country and possibly attend school to complete my master's degree. I sold my husband on the idea of why Canada would be a great place to live. It had four seasons and was very family-oriented! He saw my vision and became excited, too! We started researching and applying to schools and jobs in Ontario. We chose Ontario because my husband had family there. We applied to become permanent residents, and in the span of six months, we had our permanent residency stamped in our passports. We were going to Canada! Yes, it started out exciting. I was young, energetic, and ready to take on this new adventure.

Then, I experienced my first winter. I was excited to see snow for the first time and felt happy initially. However, that happy feeling did not last long. I realized that the winters lasted longer than I had imagined, and I was not responding well to the cold weather. I began to have a longing for the warmth of the sun that I grew up with in Jamaica. I struggled with sadness and isolation and found it challenging to function normally during winter. "After embarking on a major move to Canada, I could not move now," I told myself. "I had to be strong and deal with it."

After seven years of enduring and fighting, I realized that I was struggling with Seasonal Affective Disorder and had enlarged lymph nodes at the back of my neck. Seasonal Affective Disorder (SAD) is a type of depression that typically occurs in the fall and winter months when there is less sunlight. SAD is also known as seasonal depression or winter blues. (See Appendix I to learn more about SAD.)

I became concerned. This led me to my doctor, and they started doing tests and monitoring the growth of my lymph nodes. I was forced to face the reality that I was struggling with living in Canada during the winter months. This was very difficult to accept because I loved living in Canada and was unsure of how to approach this situation. I made the decision to meet with a mental health therapist to process my challenges and hopefully get some support. Some people may be alarmed that I was a trained therapist seeking support for counseling. It is pretty much the same as a medical doctor needing to seek medical attention if they have health challenges. During the counseling process, it was confirmed that my depression symptoms were linked to the winter months, and I would have to decide on a treatment plan. The options were to continue with therapy to help with my symptoms, increase vitamin D intake, and, if the symptoms continued, consider going on medication during the winter or relocate to somewhere that had warmer temperatures. As a family, we talked about the possible ways to move forward and decided that it would be best to move to a warmer climate. We made that decision because of the realization that I was happier and functioned better in warmer climates. We also came to the conclusion that the winters were long and consistent, and there was no way to change those facts. Consequently, I had to make the change; I had to adjust because I could not change the environment. The medication would have probably been helpful with my mood and outlook; however, we also realized that we did not like how we had to function and live during the winter months. We preferred living and functioning in a warm environment. So we assessed the evidence and our needs as a family, and moving became the clear choice. There are some people who really enjoy being outside in wintertime and eagerly look forward to the cold seasons with joy and great expectations. For us, we could only last short periods of time outside in the cold before running for refuge. The snowstorms were brutal sometimes and impacted movement. For those who have lived in cold environments, you can relate to those times when you spend hours shoveling your driveway before you go to work only to realize when you get home that you cannot drive onto your driveway because the snowplow came by and built a high wall of snow in front of your house. We truly struggled with functioning and enjoying the winter seasons. We had to implement the R.E.A.L Strategy to propel us to make the difficult decision to move.

In spite of the challenges of winter, to be honest, it was not an easy decision to leave because Ontario was now home to us. Outside of winter, we loved Ontario. We loved the people, culture, and landscape, especially in spring and summer. The decision to leave would also require us to leave our families, which included my sister, who had since migrated to Canada with her family, my husband's family, and friends. It required us to leave what was familiar to a place unknown, as we did when we had left Jamaica previously.

Additionally, at this point in my life, I had completed a master's degree in social work, had a beautiful baby girl, started my own business, and was approached about a major contract that would grow my business exponentially. However, despite what appeared to be many reasons to stay, we decided to move to Georgia after visiting and experiencing the difference in the climate. We chose Georgia because, although we wanted to return to Jamaica, the Lord revealed to us that it was not the right timing. Georgia was an excellent middle ground because it provided some comfort, knowing that it would be only a two-hour flight back to Canada and a little over a two-hour flight to Jamaica. We could visit family often and still enjoy the two countries we love, although in a limited manner.

We embarked on the journey, which took a year and a half to execute; however, we did it! Fast forward seven years later to today, and my swollen lymph nodes are almost nonexistent. I will explain later why the challenges with my lymph nodes, although drastically reduced, were not eliminated. My depression is minimal. I am happy. Going through this journey opened my eyes to the negative impact of stress on the body. I realized that making the decision to face my stressors and deal with them instead of enduring them drastically improved my health physically and mentally. I cannot say it was easy to relocate and start afresh, but I can unequivocally say it was worth it! I discovered that my peace was priceless and worth fighting for.

You may be going through a stressful period in your life right now as you read these pages, whether it be the loss of a loved one, an abusive relationship, financial worries, sickness, or just feeling a general sense of unhappiness. I want to encourage you today: things don't have to remain the way they are. With God's help, you can learn to manage your stress and overcome whatever it is that is weighing you down and preventing you from experiencing happiness and joy.

In this chapter, I will share with you some amazing, mind-blowing facts about how stress impacts our bodies. I only have one request: please do not skip this section! Knowing this information will drastically change your life. Why will it be life-changing? Because you will be learning how stress impacts ten systems in the body—yes, ten! You are going to realize that chronic stress is linked to many diseases that we all deal with as individuals. You certainly do not want to live without this type of information.

STRESS DEFINED

We have Hans Selye to thank for the commonly used word "stress." He was born in Vienna on January 26, 1907; he was Hungarian–Canadian. His father was a surgeon, and Hans became an endocrinologist and researcher through his inspiration. "Stress" was a term used in physics; however, Hans Selye introduced it in medicine. He became known as the "Father of Stress Research." Hans turned the medical community on its head when he chose to focus on universal patient reactions to illness. He recognized that illness and stress can produce similar physiological responses in the body. For example, both stress and illness can activate the hypothalamic-pituitary-adrenal (HPA) axis, leading to the release of cortisol, a stress hormone.

Generally, "universal patient reactions to illness" refers to the common physical, emotional, and behavioral responses people experience when ill. These reactions can include symptoms such as pain, fatigue, and nausea and emotional responses such as anxiety, depression, and fear.

His information on stress impacted scientific and lay communities alike in fields as diverse as endocrinology, complementary medicine, animal breeding, and social psychology.

Hans Selye's research on rats and stress involved placing them in various stressful situations to study their physiological responses. One experiment involved placing the rats on a cold roof of a medical building, which induced physical stress due to the cold environment. Another experiment involved using a revolving treadmill that required continuous running for the rats to stay upright, which induced physical and psychological stress. The findings in each experiment were the same: adrenal hyperactivity, lymphatic atrophy, and peptic ulcers.

Selye's research showed that chronic exposure to stress could lead to various diseases and disorders.[1] He coined the term "General Adaptation Syndrome" to describe the body's physiological response to stress. [2] Selye observed that when the body is exposed to a stressor, it responds in a specific way, which he characterized as a three-stage process: alarm, resistance, and exhaustion.

During the alarm stage, the body's sympathetic nervous system releases stress hormones such as adrenaline and cortisol. This stage is characterized by the "fight or flight" response as the body prepares to confront or escape from the stressor.

During the resistance stage, the body attempts to adapt to the ongoing stressor. This stage is characterized by increased hormone production and metabolic activity as the body works to maintain physiological balance.

If the stressor persists, the body eventually enters the exhaustion stage, where its resources are depleted, and it can no longer maintain physiological balance. This stage is characterized by decreased hormone production and metabolic activity as the body's ability to adapt is overwhelmed.

Selye's theory of GAS has been influential in understanding the physiological effects of stress on the body. It has been applied to a wide range of stressors, including illness, injury, and psychological stress.

In 1936, Hans Selye defined stress as "the non-specific response of the body to any demand for change."[3] This definition became widely used to help people understand stress and how it impacts the human body.

THREE MAJOR TYPES OF STRESS

Acute Stress

This is short-term stress that goes away quickly. You feel it when you slam on the brakes, have a fight with your partner, or ski down a steep slope. It helps you manage dangerous situations. It also occurs when you do something new or exciting. All people have acute stress at one time or another.

Episodic Stress

Episodic stress occurs when we experience acute stress too frequently. It often hits those who take on too much—those who feel they have both self-imposed pressure and external demands vying for their attention. In such cases, hostility and anger frequently result. Episodic stress also commonly afflicts those who worry a lot of the time, in turn resulting in anxiety and depression.

Chronic Stress

This is stress that lasts for a longer period of time. You may have chronic stress if you have money problems, an unhappy marriage, or trouble at work. Any type of stress that goes on for weeks or months is chronic stress. You can become so used to chronic stress that you don't realize it is a problem. If you don't find ways to manage stress, it may lead to health problems.

STRESSORS DEFINED

"A stressor is any event, force, or condition that results in physical or emotional stress. Stressors may be internal or external forces that require adjustment or coping."[4]

A stressor is any physical, psychological, or environmental event or condition that causes an individual's body to respond with the "fight or flight" response. Stressors can be acute, such as a sudden trauma or illness, or chronic, such as ongoing financial or relationship difficulties.

Examples of physical stressors include exposure to extreme heat or cold, physical injury, or infection. Psychological stressors include experiences such as job loss, relationship problems, or major life changes like a move or a divorce. Environmental stressors can include exposure to toxins or pollution or living in an area prone to natural disasters like hurricanes or earthquakes.

Examples of stressors include the following:

- The death of a loved one
- Divorce
- Loss of a job
- Increase in financial obligations
- Getting married
- Moving to a new home
- Chronic illness or injury
- Moving to a new country (migrating)
- Job demands
- Extreme weather

As you can see, stressors are issues we face throughout our lifetime. They are essentially unavoidable, and for this reason, we must learn how to manage them effectively. Learning to manage stressors is synonymous with learning to manage life. The reality is that life—although it has many beautiful and blissful moments—can sometimes become very difficult, unpredictable, and challenging.

Did You Know?

The stress response is the body's way of reacting to a challenge or demand (stressor). It is often referred to as the "fight or flight" response because it prepares the body to either fight or run away from a perceived threat. When the body experiences stress, it releases hormones, including adrenaline and cortisol. These hormones increase the heart rate, blood pressure, and blood sugar levels, making the body more alert and ready for action. This response can be helpful in short-term situations, such as if you need to flee from danger or if you need to be extra alert during an exam. However, if the stress response is triggered too often or lasts too long, it can harm the body and mind.

When we experience demands or pressure, our bodies react; however, our bodies also respond in different ways. It is important that we not lose sight of the word "non-specific" in the definition of stress because it sheds light on the reality that we all respond differently to stressors in our lives, so it is important to pay attention to your unique experience and avoid the urge to make comparisons between yourself and someone else.

"WHAT'S STRESS GOT TO DO WITH IT?"

What does stress have to do with not sleeping, lower back pain, shoulder pain, sleeping too much, cold, flu, hypertension, heart attack, stroke, arthritis, brain fog, heartburn, acid reflux, high cholesterol levels, anxiety, depression, fertility, cancer, irritable bowel syndrome, and chronic obstructive pulmonary disease? Have I piqued your interest? Exposure to prolonged stress has been linked to causing all the health issues listed above and more.

CHRONIC STRESS DEFINED

There are three main identified types of stress: chronic stress, acute stress, and episodic stress. However, this book will be focused on chronic stress.

According to the Yale Medicine Interdisciplinary Stress Center, chronic stress is a consistent sense of feeling pressured and overwhelmed for a long period.[5]

If you think about it, most of the time, we are somewhat aware of when we become stressed. We will say, "I am feeling stressed or overwhelmed." However, because of our lack of awareness, we think that the symptoms will disappear, and as a result, we continue living and functioning, not realizing that if we continue to feel stressed or overwhelmed for long periods, it slowly damages the systems in our bodies. Our bodies are equipped and created to handle stress in small doses; however, extended exposure may result in chronic stress symptoms.

Rajita Sinha, Ph.D., director of Yale Medicine's Interdisciplinary Stress Center, said, "We humans are very good at facing a challenge, solving a situation, or reaching out to someone to get support. We're wired to respond to stress and remove it, sometimes even automatically. But life has become more complex, and many situations don't have easy answers."[6]

This statement resonated with me, as I could relate to experiencing more complex situations without easy resolutions. I would also like to add that our stressors have truly multiplied: health issues have increased and have become more chronic, and disasters have become more frequent and intense, among other issues. Managing our struggles coupled with environmental stressors, social stressors, political stressors, and job stressors has certainly made it more difficult to avoid exposing ourselves to chronic stress.

SYMPTOMS OF CHRONIC STRESS

According to Yale Medicine Interdisciplinary Stress Center, there are cognitive, emotional, physical, and behavioral signs of chronic stress. Dr. Rajita Sinha says, "Not all four of these categories of symptoms are necessarily going to show up in one person, but if someone has three to five of these symptoms for more than several weeks, they might be suffering from chronic stress."[7] Those potential symptoms include the following:

- Aches and pains
- Insomnia or sleepiness
- A change in social behavior, such as staying in often
- Low energy
- Unfocused or cloudy thinking
- Change in appetite
- Increased alcohol or drug use
- Change in emotional responses to others
- Emotional withdrawal

Take a moment to review the symptoms above and examine whether or not you have been impacted by chronic stress symptoms.

Dr. Sinha explains further that chronic stress is linked to other conditions, both psychological and physical. These can include the following:

- Diseases such as hypertension, heart disease, obesity and metabolic syndrome, type II diabetes, and arthritis

- Addiction to alcohol, nicotine, and/or prescription drugs and behavioral-related issues, such as addiction to the internet, food, or gambling
- Mood disorders and anxiety disorders, which are common secondary diagnoses for people with chronic stress.[8]

THE IMPACT OF CHRONIC STRESS ON BODY SYSTEMS

According to the Yale Stress Institute, stress is believed to be the cause of 70% of doctor's office visits and 85% of serious chronic illnesses.[9]

I must confess that when I started researching how chronic stress impacts the body, I was truly surprised. I had a few jaw-dropping and hair-raising moments while learning how it impacts the mind and body. I am truly excited to share with you succinctly how stress impacts our bodies because, due to the volume of information, explaining the impact of stress on each of these systems in full detail would require individual books.

I will describe the impact of chronic stress on the body systems below from head to toe including: Nervous System; Respiratory System; Cardiovascular System; Endocrine System; Digestive System; Urinary System; Immune System; Musculoskeletal System; Circulatory System; Reproductive System; Integumentary System; Lymphatic System.

LET'S LOOK AT HOW CHRONIC STRESS IMPACTS THE NERVOUS SYSTEM

The nervous system is the body's communication network, responsible for sending and receiving messages throughout the body. It is made up of two main parts: the central nervous system (CNS) and the peripheral nervous system (PNS).

The CNS consists of the brain and spinal cord, while the PNS includes all the nerves connecting the CNS to the rest of the body. The nervous system controls all bodily functions, including movement, sensation, thought, and emotion.

Nerve cells, called neurons, are the basic building blocks of the nervous system. They transmit electrical signals called impulses, which travel from one neuron to another across small gaps called synapses. Chemical messengers called neurotransmitters help to transmit these signals across synapses.

Overall, the nervous system is vital to survival and helps us interact with the world around us. It allows us to move, sense, think, and feel and helps us to adapt and respond to environmental changes.

Chronic stress can significantly impact the nervous system, which controls all bodily functions and responds to changes in the environment. The stress response triggers the release of stress hormones, such as cortisol and adrenaline, which can alter the nervous system's functioning in the following ways:

Risk Factors

* **Increased activity in the sympathetic nervous system:** Chronic stress can lead to increased activity in the sympathetic nervous system, which is responsible for the body's fight-or-flight response. This can result in increased heart rate, blood pressure, and respiration, as well as the release of stress hormones.

* **Decreased activity in the parasympathetic nervous system:** Chronic stress can also lead to decreased activity in the parasympathetic nervous system, which is responsible for the body's rest-and-digest response. This can lead to digestive problems, fatigue, and reduced immunity.

* **Impaired cognitive function:** Chronic stress can impair cognitive function, including memory, attention, and decision-making abilities. This can affect academic and work performance, as well as social relationships.

* **Increased risk of mental health disorders:** Chronic stress can increase the risk of developing mental health disorders, such as anxiety and depression, by altering brain chemistry and neural pathways.

* **Structural changes in the brain:** Chronic stress can also lead to structural changes in the brain, including the shrinking of the prefrontal cortex and the enlargement of the amygdala, which can affect emotional regulation and stress responses.

To compound things, when our bodies have elevated stress levels over an extended period of time (more than a few days), the autonomic nervous system begins to accept this heightened stress level as normal. It continues to produce high levels of stress hormones well after the stressful event has passed, further compromising the immune system and impacting anxiety and digestion.

Chronic stress can impair communication between the immune system and the HPA axis (which involves the hypothalamus, pituitary gland, and adrenal glands), a complex system in the body that helps regulate stress and other functions. This impaired communication has been linked to the future development of numerous physical and mental health conditions, including chronic fatigue, metabolic disorders (e.g., diabetes and obesity), depression, and immune disorders.

Overall, chronic stress can significantly impact the nervous system, impair cognitive function, increase the risk of mental health disorders, and alter the body's stress response.

LET'S LOOK AT THE IMPACT OF CHRONIC STRESS ON THE RESPIRATORY SYSTEM

The respiratory system supplies oxygen to cells and removes carbon dioxide waste from the body. Air comes in through the nose and goes through the larynx in the throat, down through the trachea, and into the lungs through the bronchi. The bronchioles then transfer oxygen to red blood cells for circulation.

Stress and strong emotions can present with respiratory symptoms, such as shortness of breath and rapid breathing, as the airway between the nose and the lungs constricts.

Risk Factors

* **Breathing rate:** Stress can cause an increase in breathing rate, which can lead to hyperventilation and a decrease in the amount of carbon dioxide in the blood. This can cause symptoms such as dizziness and lightheadedness.

* **Asthma:** Stress can worsen asthma symptoms, such as shortness of breath and coughing. It can also trigger asthma attacks in some people.

* **Lung function:** Stress can also affect lung function, making breathing more difficult and reducing the amount of oxygen reaching the body's cells.

* **Immune response:** Stress can also affect the immune response in the respiratory system, making it more difficult for the body to fight off respiratory infections.

* **Sleep apnea:** Stress can also worsen sleep apnea, a disorder characterized by breathing pauses during sleep, leading to daytime fatigue and other problems.

This is generally not a problem for people without respiratory disease, as the body can manage the additional work and breathe comfortably. Still, psychological stressors can exacerbate breathing problems for people with pre-existing respiratory diseases, such as asthma and chronic obstructive pulmonary disease (COPD, including emphysema and chronic bronchitis).

Some studies show that acute stress—such as the death of a loved one—can actually trigger asthma attacks. In addition, the rapid breathing—or hyperventilation—caused by stress can bring on a panic attack in someone prone to panic attacks.

LET'S LOOK AT HOW CHRONIC STRESS IMPACTS THE CARDIOVASCULAR SYSTEM

The cardiovascular system, also known as the circulatory system, is a network of organs and vessels that is responsible for circulating blood throughout the body. It includes the heart, blood vessels (arteries, veins, and capillaries), and blood. The heart pumps blood through the blood vessels, transporting oxygen, nutrients, and hormones to the body's cells and organs and removing waste products, such as carbon dioxide. The cardiovascular system plays a crucial role in maintaining homeostasis, regulating body temperature, and supporting immune function. Diseases of the cardiovascular system—such as heart disease and stroke—are the leading causes of death worldwide.

Chronic stress can have a detrimental impact on the cardiovascular system. Here are some of the effects of chronic stress on the cardiovascular system.

Risks Factors

* **Increased risk of high blood pressure:** Chronic stress can cause the blood vessels to constrict, increasing blood pressure. Over time, this can contribute to the development of hypertension, which is a major risk factor for heart disease.

* **Increased risk of heart disease:** Chronic stress has been linked to an increased risk of developing heart disease, a leading cause of death worldwide.

* **Increased risk of arrhythmias:** Chronic stress can disrupt the heart's normal electrical activity and increase the risk of arrhythmias or abnormal heart rhythms.

* **Increased risk of atherosclerosis:** Chronic stress can contribute to the buildup of plaque in the arteries, increasing the risk of heart attack and stroke.

* **Impaired immune function:** Chronic stress can impair immune function, increasing the risk of infections and inflammation that can contribute to cardiovascular disease.

* **Inflammation:** Persistent chronic stress may also contribute to inflammation in the circulatory system, particularly in the coronary arteries, and this is one pathway that is thought to tie stress to a heart attack. It also appears that how a person responds to stress can affect cholesterol levels.

* **Elevated cortisol levels:** Chronic stress can also lead to elevated levels of the stress hormone cortisol, which can contribute to the development of heart disease by increasing inflammation and oxidative stress.

Oxidative stress refers to an imbalance between free radicals and antioxidants in the body. Free radicals are unstable molecules that can damage cells, proteins, and DNA, while antioxidants neutralize free radicals and protect cells from damage.

Under normal circumstances, the body can manage free radicals and keep them in balance with antioxidants. However, oxidative stress can occur when there is an excess of free radicals or a depletion of antioxidants. This can be caused by various factors, including environmental pollutants, radiation, poor diet, and chronic stress.

Overall, chronic stress can significantly and negatively impact the cardiovascular system, increasing the risk of heart disease, stroke, and other cardiovascular problems. It is important to manage stress and seek support if you are experiencing chronic stress to prevent long-term effects on the cardiovascular system.

LET'S LOOK AT HOW STRESS IMPACTS THE ENDOCRINE SYSTEM

The endocrine system is like a chemical messenger system in the body. It helps to regulate the body's functions and keep them in balance. Some examples of endocrine glands are the pituitary gland, thyroid gland, pancreas, adrenal gland, and ovaries or testes. Each gland produces specific hormones that have specific tasks. For example, the thyroid gland produces hormones that help regulate metabolism. The pancreas produces insulin to regulate blood sugar levels. The ovaries/testes produce hormones that regulate reproductive functions. Some of the ways that stress can affect the endocrine system include the following.

Risks Factors

* **Adrenal glands:** The adrenal glands produce the stress hormone cortisol. Chronic stress can lead to the overproduction of cortisol, which can have negative effects on the body, including weight gain, high blood pressure, and increased risk of heart disease.

* **Thyroid gland:** Stress can also affect the thyroid gland, which regulates metabolism. Chronic stress can lead to an imbalance in thyroid hormones, which can cause fatigue, weight gain or loss, and other symptoms.

* **Reproductive hormones:** Stress can also affect the production of reproductive hormones, leading to menstrual irregularities and infertility in women and erectile dysfunction in men.

* **Insulin:** Stress can also affect insulin production, increasing the risk of type 2 diabetes.

* **Growth hormone:** Stress can also affect the production of growth hormone, which can lead to muscle weakness, fatigue, and decreased bone density.

It's important to note that chronic stress can affect all of the endocrine glands and their functions, leading to a cascade of hormonal imbalances and ultimately leading to various health issues.

LET'S LOOK AT THE IMPACT OF CHRONIC STRESS ON THE DIGESTIVE SYSTEM

Chronic stress can significantly impact the digestive system, which breaks down food, absorbs nutrients, and eliminates waste products. Exposure to stress results in alterations of the brain-gut interactions ("brain-gut axis"), ultimately leading to the development of a broad array of gastrointestinal disorders. Some of the ways that stress can affect the digestive system include the following.

* **Gastrointestinal symptoms:** Stress can cause a variety of gastrointestinal symptoms, such as stomach cramps, diarrhea, constipation, and acid reflux. It can also lead to conditions such as irritable bowel syndrome (IBS) and inflammatory bowel disease (IBD).

* **Appetite:** Stress can also affect appetite, causing some people to overeat and others to lose their appetite. This can lead to weight gain or weight loss.

* **Gastric motility:** Stress can also slow down or speed up food movement through the digestive tract, leading to problems such as constipation or diarrhea.

* **Nutrient absorption:** Stress can also affect the body's ability to absorb nutrients from food, leading to deficiencies over time.

* **Gastric acid:** Stress can also affect production of gastric acid, leading to acid reflux and ulcers.

LET'S LOOK AT THE IMPACT OF CHRONIC STRESS ON THE URINARY SYSTEM

The urinary system, also known as the renal system, filters and eliminates waste products and excess fluids from the body. It consists of the following organs and structures. *Kidneys:* two bean-shaped organs located in the back of the abdominal cavity, responsible for filtering waste products and excess fluids from the blood. *Ureters are two tubes that connect the kidneys to the bladder and are* responsible for transporting urine from the kidneys to the bladder. *Bladder:* a muscular sac located in the pelvic area, responsible for storing urine until it is eliminated from the body. *Urethra:* a tube that connects the bladder to the external opening of the body, responsible for eliminating urine from the body.

The urinary system also includes the muscles and nerves that regulate urine release from the body. Its primary function is to maintain homeostasis by regulating the balance of water, electrolytes, and other substances in the blood.

Chronic stress can have a negative impact on the urinary system in several ways.

Risks Factors

* Urinary incontinence, which is the inability to control urination. Chronic stress can also increase the risk of urinary tract infections (UTIs) due to weakened immunity, decreased blood flow to the urinary tract, and decreased bladder capacity.

* Stress can increase urine production, leading to increased frequency and urgency of urination.

* Chronic stress can also lead to the development of kidney stones, as stress hormones can alter the balance of minerals in the body and increase the risk of stone formation.

* Stress can exacerbate existing urinary conditions such as overactive bladder, interstitial cystitis, and urinary retention.

✳ Chronic stress can lead to pelvic floor dysfunction, which can cause bladder or bowel dysfunction.

In summary, chronic stress can have a range of negative effects on the urinary system, including urinary incontinence, UTIs, increased frequency and urgency of urination, kidney stones, exacerbation of existing urinary conditions, and pelvic floor dysfunction.

LET'S LOOK AT THE IMPACT OF CHRONIC STRESS ON THE IMMUNE SYSTEM

Like a police force, our immune system deals with invaders of our bodies to protect our bodies from getting sick. Our immune system comprises billions of white blood cells (lymphocytes and phagocytes) that fight off bacteria, viruses, and cancer cells in the body.

Chronic stress can have a significant impact on the immune system, which is responsible for protecting the body from infection and disease. The stress response triggers the release of stress hormones, such as cortisol and adrenaline, which can alter the immune system's functioning in the following ways.

Risks Factors

✳ **Decreased immune cell production:** Chronic stress can suppress the production of immune cells, including T cells, B cells, and natural killer cells, making the body more susceptible to infections.

✳ **Impaired immune response:** Stress hormones can impair the immune system's ability to respond to pathogens by inhibiting the production of cytokines, which are signaling molecules that activate the immune response.

✳ **Increased inflammation:** Chronic stress can also lead to increased inflammation in the body, contributing to the development of chronic diseases, such as cardiovascular disease, diabetes, and autoimmune disorders.

* **Delayed wound healing:** Stress hormones can delay the healing of wounds by impairing the function of immune cells involved in tissue repair.

* **Increased susceptibility to viral infections:** Chronic stress can increase susceptibility to viral infections, such as the common cold and flu, by weakening the immune system's ability to fight these infections.

In summary, chronic stress can significantly impact the immune system, impairing its ability to defend the body against infections and increasing the risk of developing chronic diseases.

LET'S LOOK AT THE IMPACT OF CHRONIC STRESS ON THE MUSCULOSKELETAL SYSTEM

Your musculoskeletal system includes your bones, cartilage, ligaments, tendons, and connective tissues. Your skeleton provides a framework for your muscles and other soft tissues. Together, they support your body's weight, maintain your posture, and help you move. With sudden-onset stress, the muscles tense up all at once and then release their tension when the stress passes. Chronic stress causes the muscles in the body to be in a more or less constant state of guardedness.

Chronic stress can negatively impact the musculoskeletal system in several ways.

Risks Factors

* **Muscular tension:** Stress can cause the muscles to tense up, which can lead to pain and stiffness in the neck, shoulders, and back. This can also lead to headaches and migraines.

* **Joint pain:** Stress can cause joint inflammation, leading to pain and stiffness. This is particularly true for people with conditions such as rheumatoid arthritis or osteoarthritis.

* **Osteoporosis:** Stress can lead to a decrease in bone density, which can increase the risk of osteoporosis, which causes bones to become fragile and more prone to fractures.

* **Delayed healing:** Stress can slow down the healing process of bones, muscles, and other tissues. This can prolong recovery time from injuries and surgeries.

* **Posture issues:** Stress can lead a person to adopt poor posture, putting extra strain on the muscles and joints. This can lead to pain and discomfort.

"Hormones released during stress have a negative metabolic effect on skeletal muscle. Stress can induce an earlier decline in muscle strength, eventually leading to falls and fractures. Therefore, stress should be viewed as an independent risk factor for disability and other co-morbid conditions."[10]

LET'S LOOK AT THE IMPACT OF CHRONIC STRESS ON THE CIRCULATORY SYSTEM

Chronic stress can significantly impact the circulatory system, which delivers oxygen and nutrients to the body's cells and removes waste products. Some of the ways that stress can affect the circulatory system include the following.

Risks Factors

* **Heart rate and blood pressure:** Stress can cause an increase in heart rate and blood pressure, which can put extra strain on the heart and blood vessels. This can increase the risk of heart disease, stroke, and other cardiovascular problems.

* **Blood clotting:** Stress can also increase the risk of blood clots, which can lead to blockages in the blood vessels and increase the risk of heart attack and stroke.

* **Atherosclerosis:** Stress can also promote the build-up of plaque in the arteries (atherosclerosis), which can restrict blood flow and increase the risk of heart disease and stroke.

* **Inflammation:** Stress can also cause inflammation in the body, damaging the inner lining of the blood vessels and increasing the risk of heart disease and stroke.

* **Cholesterol:** Stress can also affect cholesterol levels in the blood, leading to an increased risk of heart disease.

LET'S LOOK AT THE IMPACT OF CHRONIC STRESS ON THE REPRODUCTIVE SYSTEM

Chronic stress can impact the reproductive system, which is responsible for producing hormones, producing eggs and sperm, and regulating the menstrual cycle in women. Some of the ways that stress can affect the reproductive system include the following.

Risks Factors

* **Menstrual cycle:** Stress can disrupt the menstrual cycle, causing irregular periods or heavy bleeding. It can also affect ovulation and fertility.

* **Hormonal changes:** Stress can cause changes in the levels of hormones produced by the reproductive system, leading to conditions such as polycystic ovary syndrome (PCOS) and endometriosis.

* **Low libido:** Stress can affect sexual desire, decreasing interest in sex.

* **Erectile dysfunction:** Stress can affect sexual function in men, leading to problems such as erectile dysfunction. Stress causes the body to release the hormone cortisol produced by the adrenal glands. Excess amounts of cortisol can affect the normal biochemical functioning of the male reproductive system.

✳ **Pregnancy and childbirth:** Stress can also affect pregnancy and childbirth, increasing the risk of complications such as preterm labor, low birth weight, and postpartum depression.

LET'S LOOK AT THE IMPACT OF STRESS ON THE INTEGUMENTARY SYSTEM

The integumentary system is the body's largest organ system and includes the skin, hair, nails, sweat glands, and oil glands. Its primary function is to provide a physical barrier to protect the body from damage and infection, regulate body temperature, and eliminate waste. The skin is composed of multiple layers and is continuously renewing itself. Hair and nails are also produced by the integumentary system and serve to protect and insulate the skin. The sweat and oil glands help to regulate body temperature and maintain skin hydration. The integumentary system also plays a role in sensory perception and vitamin D synthesis.

Risks Factors

✳ Stress can have a significant impact on the integumentary system. Psychological stress can also disrupt the epidermal barrier—the top layer of the skin that locks in moisture and protects us from harmful microbes. Chronic stress can cause skin issues such as acne, eczema, hives, psoriasis, hair loss, and nail problems.

✳ Stress can also disrupt the skin's barrier function, making it more susceptible to infections and irritants.

✳ Additionally, stress can cause changes in hormone levels that can impact the sebaceous glands and lead to oily or dry skin. Stress can also disrupt sleep, leading to dark circles and puffiness under the eyes.

✳ Finally, stress can increase the likelihood of compulsive skin-picking and nail-biting, causing further damage to the integumentary system.

LET'S LOOK AT THE IMPACT OF STRESS ON THE LYMPHATIC SYSTEM

The lymphatic system is the most extensive circulatory system in the body. The lymphatic system is our body's own waste removal service. It is the least talked about body system but arguably the most vital. A significant component of the circulatory system, twice as large as the arterial system, is a network of tissues and vessels that transport and dispose of lymphatic waste and other fluids. Its most important function is its role in our immune response: lymphocytes (white blood cells) originate from and are transported in the lymphatic system to fight off diseases and infections. Unlike the heart in the arterial system, the lymphatic system does not have an automatic pump; therefore, maintaining fluid transport in the lymph vessels requires activity and movement from us.

Risk Factors

* An impaired lymphatic system will lead to a weakened immune response, meaning we get ill more often.

* Poor lymph circulation results in inflammation or disease, so it is imperative to make lifestyle changes to keep the lymph system healthy. Exercise is the answer.

* An alkaline environment in the body is the most optimal for the drainage of the lymphatic system. When we experience stress, cortisol (a stress-fighting hormone) is released, resulting in metabolic acidosis. Cortisol's acidic nature can cause a breakdown of lymphoid tissue, suppress immune function, reduce the circulation of protective antibodies, and promote fat gain.

Becoming aware of how stress impacts the body's systems is a major step in learning how to prevent and manage chronic stress. If any of the body systems explored resonates with your experience, please continue to read this book and do further research so that you can begin the journey of becoming a healthier you.

CHAPTER 2

PART 2- HOW STRESS IMPACTS OUR BODIES –

EXPLORING THE MENTAL HEALTH IMPLICATIONS OF LONG-TERM STRESS

IN THIS CHAPTER, I WOULD LIKE TO ZERO IN ON THE IMPACT OF chronic stress on mental health and mental illnesses. If you or a loved one is struggling with mental health challenges, then this chapter will be helpful for you.

Mental health has been plagued with stigma and poor funding for years. However, since COVID-19, there has been an increase in the number of persons seeking support for mental health issues, which has resulted in increased awareness and service provisions.

According to the Stress on America 2020 report, Americans have been profoundly affected by the COVID-19 pandemic, and the external factors Americans have listed in previous years as significant sources of stress remain present and problematic. These compounding stressors have real consequences on our minds and bodies. The report revealed that nearly eight in ten adults (78 percent) say the coronavirus pandemic was a significant source of stress in their lives. Two in three adults (67 percent) say they experienced increased stress throughout the pandemic.[11]

MENTAL HEALTH VS. MENTAL ILLNESS

Mental health refers to a person's overall psychological well-being, which includes emotional, social, and cognitive functioning. It involves how we think, feel, and act. It is the state of being able to cope with the normal stresses of life, work productively, and contribute to society in a meaningful way.

On the other hand, mental illness refers to a wide range of conditions that affect a person's mental health and disrupt their normal thought processes, emotions, and behavior. Mental illness can range from mild to severe. It can significantly impact a person's quality of life, relationships, and ability to function in society.

It is important to note that mental illness does not necessarily mean a person is not mentally healthy. Mental illness is a medical condition that requires professional diagnosis and treatment. On the other hand, mental health is a state of being that requires ongoing self-care and attention to maintain.

People sometimes avoid talking about and learning more about mental health because they believe the term refers to having a mental illness. On the other hand, some people are struggling with mental illnesses that are affecting their functioning. However, they do not seek help because of the stigma of being seen as "crazy or incapable." I want to reinforce that having a mental illness, such as anxiety disorder or schizophrenia, does not mean you cannot be mentally healthy. If managed like any other health condition, such as high blood pressure or heart disease, a mentally ill person can have a normal life and healthy mental health.

CHRONIC STRESS AND MENTAL HEALTH

Chronic stress can have a significant impact on a person's mental health. Prolonged exposure to stressors can lead to the development of mental health conditions such as anxiety and depression. Some of the common impacts of chronic stress on mental health include the following.

* **Anxiety:** Chronic stress can cause unease, worry, and fear, leading to anxiety. This can result in physical symptoms like rapid heartbeat, sweating, and trembling.

* **Depression:** Chronic stress can lead to feelings of sadness, hopelessness, and lack of interest in activities that were once enjoyed. This can affect a person's ability to function and lead to decreased productivity.

* **Insomnia:** Chronic stress can make it difficult for a person to fall asleep or stay asleep, leading to insomnia. Lack of sleep can further exacerbate stress and impact mental health.

* **Substance abuse:** Chronic stress can lead to self-medicating behaviors, such as alcohol or drug abuse, to cope with the stress.

What this means is that you can be functioning normally and have great mental health until you are faced with a major stressor, such as COVID-19 or the death of a loved one, and begin experiencing symptoms that could indicate a mental illness. If you realize that your mood has become unstable—for example, you are feeling more sadness or emptiness, and it is impacting your desire to engage in your usual activities for over two weeks or more—it could be an indicator that you might be developing a mental illness that needs professional attention.

It is critical to understand the impact that chronic stress can have on our mental health to increase our awareness and welfare.

CHRONIC STRESS AND MENTAL ILLNESS

Chronic stress can significantly impact the development and exacerbation of mental illnesses. When the body is exposed to prolonged stress, it can trigger the release of hormones that affect the brain and body. This can lead to changes in mood, behavior, and physical health. Some of the common impacts of chronic stress on mental illness include the following.

* **Increased risk of developing mental illness:** Chronic stress can increase the risk of developing mental illnesses, such as anxiety disorders, depression, and post-traumatic stress disorder (PTSD). The longer the stress persists, the greater the risk of developing a mental illness.

* **Exacerbation of existing mental illness:** Chronic stress can worsen the symptoms of existing mental illnesses. For example, a person with anxiety may experience more frequent and severe panic attacks when exposed to chronic stressors.

* **Impaired cognitive function:** Chronic stress can impair cognitive function, such as memory, attention, and decision-making. This can further impact a person's ability to manage and cope with their mental illness.

* **Substance abuse:** Chronic stress can increase the likelihood of substance abuse as a coping mechanism for managing mental illness symptoms.

* **Physical health problems:** Chronic stress can lead to physical health problems that can worsen mental illness symptoms. For example, chronic pain can exacerbate symptoms of depression.

If you are diagnosed with a mental health disorder, you may notice that your symptoms sometimes worsen when faced with a major stressor, although you are compliant with your medication. This is because chronic stress can cause chemical changes in the brain that may result in your symptoms increasing from moderate to severe. If this is happening to you, don't be scared or panic; talk with your treating doctor, create a new plan forward, and then find ways to manage the stressor if possible.

If you can't change or manage the stressor, then the next step is to change and manage yourself.

A BIBLICAL PERSPECTIVE

Solomon in the Bible spoke about the impact of stress on our emotional health many years ago in the book of Proverbs. He stated, "Anxiety in the heart of man causes depression, but a good word makes it glad" (Proverbs 12:25 NKJV). The impact of worrying about life on the body is not new or unique to us. Through His prophets and inspired men, God revealed to us that stress can cause us to become anxious and depressed. Stressors can cause us to worry, and when we worry, it causes us to become overwhelmed and sad. I call them the three BFFs (Best, Friends, For life): stress, anxiety, and depression; they are always together.

Science has, in recent times, confirmed Solomon's statement. Neuroscientists at Harvard Medical School and its affiliate McLean Hospital have shown that long-term exposure to stress hormones in mice directly results in the anxiety that often comes with depression. After years of circumstantial evidence linking stress and depression, this evidence may be the "smoking gun" of what causes some types of mood disorders.[12]

Scientists already knew that many people with depression have high levels of cortisol, a human stress hormone. Still, it wasn't clear whether that was a cause or effect. Now it appears likely that long-term exposure to cortisol actually contributes to the symptoms of depression.

Paul Ardayfio, PhD candidate, and Kwang-Soo Kim, PhD, of the Molecular Neurobiology Laboratory at McLean Hospital, discovered this by exposing mice to both short-term and long-term durations of stress hormones, which in rodents is corticosterone. In humans, usually ongoing, chronic stress, such as caring for a spouse with dementia, rather than acute stress, has been associated with depression.

Using fifty-eight mice, the researchers gave the hormone in drinking water so as not to confound the results with the stress of injection. Chronic doses were seventeen to eighteen days of exposure; acute doses were twenty-four hours of exposure.

Compared with mice given stress hormones for a day, mice given stress hormones for more than two weeks took significantly longer to emerge from a small dark compartment into a brightly lit open field, a common behavioral test of anxiety in animals. In other words, they seemed more fearful and were less willing to explore the new environment. Chronic but not acute treatment also dulled reactions to a startling stimulus, another sign that their nervous systems were overwhelmed.[13] This research revealed that chronic stress can cause anxiety and depression.

Please note that not all mental health challenges or illnesses are stress-related. Some people experience mental health challenges because they inherited it and have a predisposition. Mental illness can be passed on in the genes as any other illness.

I will go out on a limb and say there is not a human family on the earth that has not witnessed or experienced mental health challenges or illnesses. Once we are living and breathing, we will struggle with health and mental health predispositions, and we will struggle with the potential exposure to chronic stress. We may not want to acknowledge it because of the stigma; however, it does not change the fact that it exists.

Throughout my professional career as a mental health therapist, I have seen people hurt themselves and their families and rob themselves of happy lives and fulfilled dreams because of avoiding seeking help because of stigma. My hope and passion are to normalize mental health challenges and to help people seek support early before it is too late.

Managing our stress is most certainly not optional; it physically impacts our minds and bodies. Chronic stress can seriously impact our mental health and well-being. The reality is that stressors and stress will always be with us; however, managing stress is the key to a happy life.

Who knew that chronic stress could contribute to many of the health issues we face? God knew! Our Creator knew that life's challenges could destroy our organs and cause us not to have a healthy mind and body.

Proverbs 17:22 is a short Bible verse; however, it holds valuable lessons for life that I think many of us might not have paid attention to. It says, "A merry heart doeth good like medicine: but a broken spirit dries up the bones" (KJV). Let's unpack this text for a minute. Just being happy heals our bodies. And on the flip side, sadness and worrying can cause death. Dried bones are dead; there is no life in them. Take a minute to just process that and let it sink in. Profound.

We just learned from reviewing how stress impacts our bodies that the same hormone, cortisol, that gives us energy and metabolism and helps produce vital hormones to give clarity, memory, and happiness, is the same hormone that becomes detrimental to most of our body systems when we are exposed to stress over a long period.

The reality is that stress cannot be avoided. Stressors are woven into the very fabric of our daily lives. Because of sin, death is inevitable, as well as natural disasters, crises in the world, pain and abuse in our families, sickness, and the uncertainty of life; I could go on listing for days the stressors that are in our control and out of our control.

So, what should we do? How do you navigate this world? Here is a suggested option: Learn how to navigate our stressors, how to manage what life throws at us daily, and most importantly, how to have the God factor in our life equation.

God factor: We depend on God to help us manage and overcome challenges; we receive God's healing power. It is choosing to do life with God to experience the effects of living with the supernatural element. Learning how to manage our stressors with the help of God will lead to a life of peace and abundance of happiness amid life's challenges.

I hope you feel more informed after reading about how stress impacts the body. You might even be surprised about how vast and impactful chronic stress is on our bodies and, by extension, our lives. I hope you have revelations about your body and how you may have been impacted.

Is it possible to have a healthy, fulfilling, happy life without learning how to manage stress?

With the R.E.A.L. Stress Management Strategy, you are going to learn practical steps on how to manage your stress and create a life that is happy in a world that is filled with uncertainties and difficulties.

CHAPTER 3

THE R.E.A.L. STRESS MANAGEMENT STRATEGY EXPLAINED

It's not stress that kills us; it is our reaction to it.

– Hans Selye

R.E.A.L. IS AN ACRONYM FOR R: RECOGNIZING YOUR SYMPTOMS; E: education about how to manage your symptoms; A: adjusting your life to include the things that help you to manage your stress; and L (Live, Love, Laugh): living and maintaining a life that will allow you to continue to be healthy and happy.

The first part of this approach focuses on increasing awareness of your symptoms. There is a phrase that has always stuck with me throughout life. I am not sure if I created it or heard it somewhere; however, it is profound and says, "We cannot fix what we do not understand." The more we learn and understand something, the more it places us in a position to effectively change it. If you notice that your pipe is leaking water, although you turned it off, the first thing you are going to do is explore what is causing the leak. You will not be able to fix that leak if you do not examine the source of the leak. Once you have discovered the source of the leak, the next thing you will probably do is try to fix it. Based on what you have learned, you will have to ask yourself, "Can I fix this problem? Do I have the ability and resources?" If you have the ability and resources, then you will fix it, and your leak will be resolved. If you have no idea how to fix it, you would probably seek out someone with more expertise—maybe after trying to fix it on your own for hours or maybe days.

The R and E in the R.E.A.L. approach focuses on increasing awareness about you and how you respond to stress. It also focuses on learning multiple strategies and coping mechanisms on how to reduce and manage how stress impacts you. Although we share commonalities, we are all unique. We come from different backgrounds and cultures and have different genes, dispositions, and family histories. Because of these complexities, it is important that we take the time to learn about ourselves. Learn about what makes us happy and what causes us discomfort or distress.

Learning is one milestone; the next level is knowing how to support ourselves with strategies that help us function effectively in our daily lives while navigating challenges. In this book, you will learn about stressors, how to identify your stressors, how to identify your symptoms, coping strategies, and how to use coping strategies to manage and reduce your stress.

The second part of the R.E.A.L. approach, A and L, focuses on making the necessary adjustments and changes to achieve happiness while learning how to maintain your balance and happiness.

The A is for adjust. The truth is that knowing something is a big step! However, it does not end there; the next step is doing something with the knowledge. Change can be very challenging for a lot of people because it's an unknown space. We sometimes become very comfortable in situations that cause us great stress—the lack of sleep and can't eat kind of stress, and we tell ourselves that it's better to stay with what we know than to explore an unknown territory because it could be worse. Sometimes, changes cause us to lose things or people we care about, and that's scary. Sometimes, change feels very uncomfortable. Sometimes, we just can't find the motivation to do what we know will make us happier and healthier. For most of my life, I honestly believed that change was negative because I felt discomfort or pain when a change occurred. However, I soon realized that change was inevitable. We were created to change. Think about it: if our bodies did not change, we would remain babies. It required growth and development for us to move from infancy to adulthood. We would not have a population; I probably would not be here. If the plants did not change to get rid of their dead leaves and form new roots and branches, we would not have food or beautiful flowers. I dare say change is normal. Some changes bring joy, and some changes bring tears and pain. The truth is we cannot experience growth without change; it's just not possible. Have we been misled to believe that trying to control things and keep them the same would make us happier? I hope that you, like me, will be awakened to the reality that change is normal and cannot be avoided. The key is learning how to navigate life stressors and adjust based on what our body and mind indicate we need to stay afloat. The reality is that change requires much prayer, motivation, and courage. In this book, you will learn some key strategies for embracing and navigating change instead of avoiding it.

Lastly, the L stands for live, love, and laugh. We need to live and maintain a happy life. We see the words live, love, and laugh a lot on mugs, wall decals, and bumper stickers. There is no question that living, loving, and laughing are critical actions we need to be engaged in to have a happy life. However, it can be very challenging to implement them when we are experiencing stressors and challenges. Some might think having a happy life is a pie-in-the-sky idea; however, I want to let you know that it is possible! Why? Because God our Creator said that He came to this earth for us to have life—not just an ordinary life but one with an abundance of peace, love, and laughter. Take a look at this text in John 10:10 (NKJV); it says, "The thief does not come except to steal, and to kill, and to destroy. I have come that they may have life and that they may have *it* more abundantly." A happy life is promised to us; however, we can only receive it if we follow Christ. David writes about finding joy and experiencing the pleasures of this life and eternity in Psalm 16:11 (NKJV): "You will show me the path of life; In Your presence *is* fullness of joy; At Your right hand are pleasures forevermore."

After you have worked on creating the necessary changes to feel happy and fulfilled, maintaining the changes is the next step. Changes may involve a new job, moving to a new country or neighborhood, a new mindset, implementing activities for a healthy lifestyle, new relationships, or more time with God. Whatever the change, it requires maintenance for you to continue to enjoy the benefits of adjusting.

There are a lot of things that can derail you from your routine; some are in your control, and some things are outside of your control. For example, things outside of our control could be the loss of a loved one, natural disasters impacting some aspect of our lives and functioning, being laid off, or experiencing trauma and pain in our childhoods. Things in our control, for example, could be choosing not to go the gym or connecting with people in your life because you are feeling stressed out and overwhelmed.

Life is not perfect, and we are not perfect; I have yet to meet a perfect person. Have you? We are just human beings with vulnerabilities and strengths, trying to create a fulfilling life with the help of God while navigating whatever life throws at us.

Because of this imperfection, we have to learn to be kind to ourselves when we are experiencing challenges and things are not going as planned. We have to learn steps to reflect, revisit, and reorder our lives with the help of God.

This book offers helpful tips on maintaining happiness as an imperfect person living in an imperfect world.

CHAPTER 4

R—RECOGNIZE YOUR SYMPTOMS:

THE POWER OF SELF-AWARENESS

If you ask what is the single most important key to longevity,
I would have to say it is avoiding worry, stress and tension.
And if you didn't ask me, I'd still have to say it.

– George Burns

STEP ONE IN THE R.E.A.L. STRESS MANAGEMENT APPROACH focuses on increasing self-awareness. What are your stressors? What are your stress symptoms and signals?

In Chapter 1, I mentioned speaking more about the lymph nodes behind my neck. After I realized that reducing my stressors caused my lymph node swelling to reduce, I began to notice that when I became overwhelmed and felt stressed, my neck lymph nodes would become slightly swollen again. I came to the realization that it was a stress signal. Another stress signal I noticed was musculoskeletal pain in my shoulders. I recognized that if I ignored the pain, it would intensify. I also recognized that once I implemented my stress management strategies that were unique to me my needs, my symptoms would significantly subside or disappear completely. So, over the years, I have learned that depending on what type of stressors I was experiencing and how I responded to these stressors,

I would experience certain symptoms—pain in my shoulders, a swollen lymph node in my neck, difficulty focusing on and completing tasks, and irritability. These symptoms became my stress signals. By recognizing your stressors, stress symptoms, and signals, you can take steps to manage your stress more effectively.

In this chapter, you will participate in activities to increase your awareness of your stressors, stress symptoms, and signals. Now is the perfect time for you to take a stress test.

ASSESSMENT OF YOUR PERCEIVED STRESS

Indicate with a check mark how often you felt or thought a certain way during the last month.

	0=Never	1=Almost Never	2=Sometimes	3=Fairly Often	4=Very Often
1. In the last month, how often have you felt that you were unable to control the important things in your life?					
2. In the last month, how often have you NOT felt confident about your ability to handle your personal problems?					
3. In the last month, how often have you felt that things were NOT going your way?					
4. In the last month, how often have you felt as if difficulties were piling up so high that you could not overcome them?					
Total Score					

Table 1- Source: Yale Stress Center - Perceived Stress Scale - Created by Sheldon Cohen et al

Table 1 – Source: Yale Stress Center – Perceived Stress Scale – Created by Sheldon Cohen et al

Scoring: Total up the scores for items/columns 1–4 above.

Higher scores denote greater current stress. Keep a log to compare your scores from month to month.[14]

PHYSICAL SIGNS AND SYMPTOMS

Check in with your body's stress signals. These can serve as warning signs that the situation you are dealing with is overwhelming, uncontrollable, and highly stressful.

Have you felt any of the changes listed below in your body and mind when you are facing a high-stress situation?	Yes	No
1. Heart changes (heart quickens; heart beats faster; heart races; heart skips a beat; heart pounding; pain in chest)		
2. Changes in breathing (breathing faster; breathing slower; gasping for air; shallow breathing; labored breathing)		
3. Stomach changes (cramps in the stomach; stomach in a knot; butterflies in the stomach; heavy feeling in stomach; sensation of having a bowel movement)		
4. Muscle tension (head pounding; headaches; tightness in face; tightness in jaw; feel tense all over; tension in back, neck, arms, or legs; flushed face; tension in forehead; tension in shoulders)		
5. Fear and anxiety (jitteriness; whole body is shaky; feel restless; irritable; hands trembling; want to run and escape)		
6. Sad and depressed feelings (eyes watering; feeling choked up; lump in your throat; feel like crying; feeling empty, drained, or hollow; deep intense pain sensation; hurts to be alive; tears come to your eyes; feelings are dulled)		

Have you felt any of the changes listed below in your body and mind when you are facing a high-stress situation?	Yes	No
7. Anger feelings (clenched jaw; grit your teeth; clenched fists; eyes burning; blood rushes to your head; want to smash something; want to scream and strike someone)		
8. Sweat and perspiration changes (feel sweaty; sweat pours out; feel hot all over; palms are clammy; beads of perspiration; dry mouth)		
9. Sensations in chest (sinking feeling in chest; constriction in the chest; heaviness in the chest)		
10. Cognitive/mental state changes (losing focus and concentration; increased distraction; loss of memory and forgetfulness; loss of energy; fatigue or tiredness)		
11. Changes in urges or cravings and intake (increased urge for cigarettes, alcoholic drinks; caffeine, comfort foods; overeating; overdrinking, loss of appetite)		
12. Sleep changes (insomnia; frequent waking; difficulty falling or staying asleep; early waking)		
13. Other changes (increased aches and pains in joints; increased frequency of colds, other signs specific to you)		
Total Count		

Table 2: Source: Yale Stress Center – Perceived Stress Scale –
Created by Sheldon Cohen et al

Scoring: The more changes you say yes to, the greater the impact stress has on your body and mind.

Now that you have become aware of your stress level, the next step is to take some time to identify your specific stressors.

SELF-AWARENESS, PART 1

Know Your Stressors – Stressor Defined

A stressor is any physical or psychological factor that causes stress or strain on an individual, such as a major life change, a difficult work environment, financial problems, health challenges, or a traumatic event. Stressors can be acute (short-term) or chronic (long-term), and they can be external (such as a stressful event or situation) or internal (such as negative self-talk or worry). Stressors activate the body's stress response, triggering a range of physical and emotional reactions designed to help the body cope with the perceived threat or challenge.

Identifying your stressors can be a very triggering process. Depending on the stressor, it could cause you to experience flashbacks of negative experiences or experience physical symptoms that can be very uncomfortable. If you find this process difficult, you need professional support from a trained therapist to help you explore and manage your challenges effectively. Please don't avoid the process or beat yourself up. Remember, our bodies send us signals to help us navigate life. Feeling overwhelmed is just a signal that you need support. With the proper support, you can learn ways to eventually manage your challenges on your own. (Please check out Appendix II for tips to finding the best therapist for you.)

Take a few minutes and think about your stressors. What keeps you up at night? What concerns or worries replay consistently in your thoughts and mind daily? What causes your chest to tighten or your belly to become uneasy when you see it or think about it? What is the last thing you think about before going to bed, and the first thing you think about when you wake up? We need to pay attention to and notice the things that disrupt our peace, our sleep, our mood, and our overall functioning because knowing your stressors is the first critical step in changing how they impact your life.

We sometimes neglect to pay attention to our stressors for many reasons, including not understanding the importance of identifying them. We are too busy to notice them. We may think that our time would be better spent addressing other things than trying to identify them. Or noticing them may cause more stress because of their complex nature.

I have some news for you today: Ignoring our stressors doesn't make them go away; they still impact us. However, we can manage how they impact us if we learn to identify them.

Here is a checklist to help you identify your stressors. If you have stressors that are not on the list, please add them in the extra spaces provided.

CHECKLIST TO HELP IDENTIFY YOUR STRESSORS

- ☐ Work-related stressors: high workload, tight deadlines, a toxic work environment, lack of control over work tasks or schedules, difficult co-workers or bosses, etc.
- ☐ Financial stressors: lack of savings, debt, unexpected expenses, job loss or insecurity, etc.
- ☐ Relationship stressors: conflicts with partners, family members, or friends; communication issues; lack of social support, etc.
- ☐ Health-related stressors: chronic illness or pain, disability, injuries, insomnia, poor nutrition, etc.
- ☐ Lifestyle stressors: lack of exercise, overeating, smoking, substance abuse, social media addiction, etc.
- ☐ Environmental stressors: noise, pollution, traffic, extreme weather, etc.
- ☐ Life events stressors: divorce, death of a loved one, moving, pregnancy or childbirth, etc.
- ☐ Personal stressors: negative self-talk, perfectionism, low self-esteem, etc.
- ☐ Societal stressors: a pandemic, mass shootings, racial tension, political tension, etc.

Use **Appendix III** to write out your individual stressors.

By identifying your stressors, you can better understand your sources of stress and take steps to manage them more effectively.

SELF-AWARENESS, PART 2

Now that you have identified your stressors, I want you to focus on part 2 of your self-awareness journey: knowing how stress impacts your body, emotions, and mind. You have learned so far that stress impacts almost all of the body's systems and functions. However, one person may not experience all stress symptoms; you may experience one symptom or many symptoms. Knowing your stress symptoms is crucial in managing your stress.

STRESS SIGNAL DEFINED

A stress signal is a physical or behavioral indicator that an individual is experiencing stress. Stress signals can vary depending on the individual and the level of stress they are experiencing, but some common physical stress signals include increased heart rate, rapid breathing, muscle tension, sweating, and digestive problems. Behavioral stress signals can include changes in appetite or sleep patterns, irritability, social withdrawal, and decreased productivity. Stress signals can serve as warning signs that an individual is under too much stress and needs to take steps to manage it before it becomes chronic and leads to negative health outcomes.

Imagine you driving on the road, and the sign says, "If you feel your car jerking and the road is no longer smooth, you are entering a danger zone and may fall over a cliff." Would you stop? Or would you keep going?

These symptoms/signals you are experiencing are your body's way of telling you that your stress hormones, such as cortisol, are too high and will harm your body if you do not reduce them. If you continue doing the things you are doing without stopping to identify and manage the problem, the symptoms will become more chronic and result in serious life-altering illnesses or maybe death.

KNOW YOUR STRESS SIGNALS AND SYMPTOMS

I would like you to review the checklist and identify symptoms that are specific to you. How does stress impact your body? Is it your shoulder, back, or migraine? Is it your sleep? Is it your mood? Your digestive system?

Review the list and check the boxes that apply to you. If you do not see what you experience on the list, write it down. This might be your first time investigating your stress response, so be patient with yourself. If you do not notice anything immediately, take a break from the list for a couple of days or a week; be intentional about noticing changes in your mind, mood, and body, and then revisit the list.

CHECKLIST TO HELP PEOPLE IDENTIFY THEIR STRESS SYMPTOMS

- ☐ Physical symptoms: headaches, muscle tension, stomachaches, chest pain, palpitations, fatigue, high blood pressure, etc.

- ☐ Emotional symptoms: anxiety, depression, irritability, mood swings, restlessness, etc.

- ☐ Behavioral symptoms: changes in appetite, sleep disturbances, substance abuse, social withdrawal, procrastination, increased intake of Over-the-Counter medication (OTC) and prescription pain pills, etc.

- ☐ Cognitive symptoms: memory problems, poor concentration, forgetfulness, negative thinking, racing thoughts, etc.

- ☐ Interpersonal symptoms: conflicts with others, poor communication, isolation, aggression, etc.

- ☐ Work-related symptoms: poor productivity, absenteeism, presenteeism, reduced creativity, etc.

- ☐ Spiritual symptoms: loss of meaning, a decreased sense of purpose, hopelessness, etc.

- ☐ _____

☐ _____

☐ _____

☐ _____

By recognizing your stress symptoms, you can take steps to manage them more effectively. Knowing your unique stressors and stress symptoms is the first step in learning how to manage stress effectively. This journey of self-discovery can lead to a happy, fulfilling, and balanced life if you choose to engage in this process.

Now that you have identified your stressors and stress symptoms, we will explore "E – Educate" in the R.E.A.L stress management strategy.

CHAPTER 5
E – EDUCATE:
PART 1 – TECHNIQUES AND TOOLS FOR STRESS REDUCTION

There is no such thing as a stress-free life. No evidence has ever been presented that suggests that a stress-free life can ever be achieved. Stress can be managed, relieved, and lessened, but never eliminated.

– Gudjon Bergmann

I AM VERY EXCITED ABOUT THIS CHAPTER BECAUSE UNDERstanding a problem is one thing. Understanding gives insight and information. However, it does not fix the problem. You have to create a plan and strategy to address the problem.

In this chapter, you will learn a lot of strategies to manage and cope with your stressors to reduce your stress symptoms. Facing our problems requires a lot of courage because it can be a challenging, anxiety-provoking, daunting, and overwhelming process at times. I want to validate you and commend you on taking the first step to face your giants by identifying your stressors and stress signals/symptoms. Before you begin Step 2, I want to remind you that you are not alone; God is with you. A beautiful text in Isaiah reminds us of God's character and His adoration, love, and support for us when we are going through challenging situations. When you read this text from Isaiah 43:1–4 (NLT), I want you to personalize it by placing your name on all the lines below.

"You Are Mine"

But now, O, _(Enter your name)_, listen to the Lord who created you.

O _(Enter your name)_, the one who formed you, says,

"Do not be afraid, for I have ransomed you.

I have called you by name; you are mine.

When you go through deep waters,

I will be with you.

When you go through rivers of difficulty,

you will not drown.

When you walk through the fire of oppression,

you will not be burned up;

the flames will not consume you.

For I am the Lord, your God,

the Holy One of Israel, your Savior.

I traded their lives for yours

because you are precious to me.

You are honored, and I love you."

I hope you feel God's arms encircling you as you read these verses because He is the same God today, yesterday, and forever.

In this chapter, you will review coping strategies to calm your heart and your mind. You will learn ways to relax, address your challenges effectively, and have positive behaviors that will help you have a healthy mind and body.

We need to understand the impact stress has on our brains because it gives insight into why we struggle to make the best decisions and experience changes in our moods and memories when the demands of life become challenging.

THE IMPACT OF STRESS ON THE BRAIN

Stress can negatively impact the gray matter in our nervous system, including the brain and spinal cord. Gray matter contains cell bodies, dendrites, and synapses of neurons, and it plays an important role in cognitive function, including perception, memory, and decision-making.

Research has shown that chronic stress can decrease the volume of gray matter in certain areas of the brain, such as the prefrontal cortex, hippocampus, and amygdala. These areas of the brain regulate emotions, memory formation, and decision-making, among other functions.

One study published in the journal *Nature Neuroscience* found that individuals who experienced chronic stress had a smaller hippocampus, a key brain region involved in memory and learning.[15] Other studies have found that chronic stress can lead to changes in the structure and function of the prefrontal cortex, which can negatively impact decision-making and impulse control.

The image below, published by the Yale Stress Center, shows a stressed brain and a relaxed brain. The image on the left is a stressed brain. The image on the right shows a relaxed brain.[16]

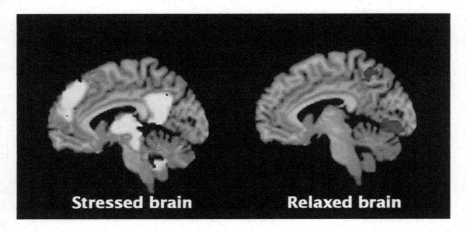

Stressed brain   Relaxed brain

Chronic stress impacts our ability to function optimally. The harsh reality is that most of the time, we deal with the demands of life and try to accomplish our goals with a brain that is not in its healthiest form. This may result in us not achieving the goals we desire, which causes us to become even more stressed, increasing the negative impact on the gray matter in our brain; it becomes cyclical.

At this point, you may ask yourself, "How do I break this cycle? How do I manage my stress to perform at my optimal level and get the desired outcome?"

I have good news for you! You have begun the process of managing your stress by being more aware of the impact of stress on your brain and body, identifying your stressors, and knowing your stress signals and symptoms.

Research shows that when our brains are not relaxed, our functioning is impaired; therefore, the next crucial step in managing stress is learning to relax your brain.

THE BENEFITS OF RELAXATION ON THE BRAIN

Relaxation can have several benefits for the brain when feeling stressed, including the following.

* **Reduced cortisol levels:** Cortisol is a hormone released during the stress response, and chronic stress can lead to chronically elevated cortisol levels, which can negatively affect the brain. Relaxation techniques, such as deep breathing or meditation, have been shown to reduce cortisol levels and improve overall well-being.

* **Increased blood flow and oxygenation:** Stress can cause blood vessels to constrict, which can reduce blood flow and oxygenation to the brain. Relaxation techniques, such as progressive muscle relaxation or guided imagery, can help to increase blood flow and oxygenation to the brain, improving cognitive function and mood.

✳ **Improved mood and mental health:** Chronic stress can lead to mood disorders, such as anxiety and depression; relaxation techniques have been shown to improve mood and overall mental health. Relaxation techniques can also help reduce symptoms of conditions such as post-traumatic stress disorder (PTSD) and obsessive-compulsive disorder (OCD).

✳ **Improved sleep:** Stress can cause difficulty falling or staying asleep, negatively impacting overall brain function. Relaxation techniques can improve sleep quality and duration, improving cognitive function, memory, and overall well-being.

Relaxation when feeling stressed can have several positive effects on the brain and overall health. Incorporating relaxation techniques into a daily routine can effectively manage stress and improve overall well-being.

In this section, you will be provided with a menu of relaxation techniques to try and see which works best for you. Complete the checklist at the end of the section to identify which relaxation technique/strategy works for you.

RELAXATION TECHNIQUES MENU

Prayer

Prayer is communication with God and then experiencing the effects of His presence in our lives. How do I know that prayer is an effective technique for relaxation? I know because God is our Creator, and He knows exactly what we need; I also know because He says he will calm our hearts and minds in the Bible, specifically Philippians 4:6–7 (NLT), which says, "Don't worry about anything; instead, pray about everything. Tell God what you need and thank him for all he has done. Then, you will experience God's peace, which exceeds anything we can understand. His peace will guard your hearts and minds as you live in Christ Jesus."

The original Greek word used in Philippians 4:7 for *guard* is φρουρέω (phroureó), which means to guard or protect. In the context of the verse, the word is used metaphorically to describe the peace of God as something that guards or protects the hearts and minds of believers in Christ Jesus.

This verse promises that if we trust in God and seek His peace, He will protect our brains from the negative impact of stress on our gray matter. After learning about the biological impact of chronic stress on the brain, this verse had a deeper meaning for me. It reinforced my belief in God as my Creator because now I have a true appreciation for why my mind needs protecting, why I need to have peace, and why I need to trust God to help manage challenges in my life. Now we know that the protection of our minds was not a random or feel-good statement. God knew exactly what we needed because He is our Creator. He knew that relaxation (peace) protected us from the negative impact of stress.

The word *guard* in this verse suggests a sense of watchfulness and protection, as if God's peace is a shield that stands guard over our thoughts and emotions. It's a reminder that we don't have to face life's challenges alone, but rather, we can turn to God for comfort and protection.

Amazingly, science has only recently started discovering the impact of stress on the brain, while the Bible was written many centuries ago and holds the remedy for your restless minds—God.

Whenever you start to feel the negative impact of stress, pray first. Tell God what troubles you, thank Him in advance, and allow Him to give you His peace so that your brain can relax.

When Prayer Is Hard

Have you ever been in a place where you could not find the words to pray or had no desire to speak to God? I know that I have. It is a very difficult space to be in; however, God knew that those days would come, so He sent the Holy Spirit, the Comforter. Romans 8:26 says the Spirit [comes to us and] helps us in our weakness. So when we do not know what to pray or how to pray the Spirit Himself [knows our need and at the right time] intercedes on our behalf with sighs and groanings too deep for words. So, when you're feeling weak, trust that God will be your strength.

Request Prayer From a Friend

Request prayer from someone you know who has a connection to God and will pray for you. If you are not comfortable sharing your concerns in detail with your friend, that's okay; be honest. Let them know you would like to be prayed for, but you are not ready to share the details of your needs.

Request Prayer from Your Church Community

There is a popular saying in the Christian community: "More prayer! More power!" These are not just words; God responds when we intercede for each other. Reach out to your spiritual community for prayer.

Deep Breathing

I believe deep breathing is one of the most underestimated strategies for relaxation. It appears to be very simple, and sometimes people say it seems silly. However, this simple act of inhaling and exhaling methodically provides many benefits to the brain and body.

Deep breathing can reduce the heart rate by activating the parasympathetic nervous system, which is responsible for slowing down the heart rate and promoting relaxation.

When we breathe deeply, we activate the diaphragm muscle, which sends a message to the brain to activate the parasympathetic nervous system. This, in turn, causes the heart rate to slow down and the blood vessels to dilate, which can help to lower blood pressure.

Deep breathing can also reduce the levels of stress hormones, such as cortisol and adrenaline, which can contribute to a faster heart rate. By promoting relaxation and reducing stress, deep breathing can help to regulate the heart rate and promote a sense of calm.

Research has shown that deep breathing exercises, such as slow and deep diaphragmatic breathing, can effectively reduce heart rate variability and promote cardiovascular health. Regular practice of deep breathing exercises can help to improve heart rate variability and reduce the risk of heart disease and other cardiovascular conditions.

Deep breathing can have several benefits on the brain and heart, including the following:

* **Reducing stress and anxiety:** Deep breathing triggers the relaxation response in the body, which can help reduce stress hormone levels such as cortisol and adrenaline. This, in turn, can reduce feelings of anxiety and promote a sense of calm.

* **Improving cognitive function:** Deep breathing can improve cognitive function by increasing blood flow and oxygen to the brain, which can help to enhance memory, attention, and concentration.

* **Lowering blood pressure:** Deep breathing can help to lower blood pressure by slowing down the heart rate and promoting relaxation.

* **Improving heart rate variability:** Deep breathing can improve heart rate variability, which is an indicator of the heart's ability to adapt to changing conditions. A healthy heart rate variability has been linked to a reduced risk of heart disease and other cardiovascular conditions.

* **Promoting relaxation and sleep:** Deep breathing can help to promote relaxation and improve sleep quality by reducing stress and anxiety and promoting feelings of calm.

Overall, deep breathing can positively impact both the brain and heart by reducing stress and promoting relaxation, which can help to improve overall health and well-being.

Steps to Do Deep Breathing Effectively

1. Find a comfortable and quiet place to sit or lie down. You can sit cross-legged on the floor, sit in a chair, or lie down on your back.

2. Place one hand on your belly and the other hand on your chest. This will help you to feel the movement of your breath.

3. Take a slow and deep breath through your nose. As you inhale, allow your belly to expand and fill with air. Try to breathe in slowly for a count of four.

4. Hold your breath for a second or two at the top of the inhale.

5. Slowly exhale through your mouth. As you exhale, allow your belly to contract, and push out the air. Try to exhale slowly for a count of four.

6. Pause for a second or two at the end of the exhale before taking another deep breath in.

7. Continue to breathe deeply in this way for several minutes. Try to focus on your breath and let go of any distracting thoughts or worries.

8. After several minutes, slowly return to your normal breathing pattern.

Scan the QR code below to watch a helpful video:

It's important to remember that deep breathing can be practiced at anytime, anywhere, and for any duration that feels comfortable. You can also experiment with different breathing patterns, such as longer inhales or exhales, to find what works best for you.

PROGRESSIVE RELAXATION

Progressive relaxation is a relaxation technique that involves tensing and releasing different muscle groups in the body in a specific order. The benefits of progressive relaxation include the following:

* **Reduced muscle tension:** Progressive relaxation can help to release tension and promote relaxation in the muscles throughout the body, reducing muscle pain and stiffness.

* **Reduced stress and anxiety:** Progressive relaxation can help to reduce feelings of stress and anxiety by promoting relaxation and calming the mind.

* **Improved sleep:** Progressive relaxation can help to improve sleep by reducing physical and mental tension that can interfere with sleep quality.

* **Improved mood:** Progressive relaxation can help improve mood by reducing stress and anxiety and promoting a sense of calm and well-being.

* **Increased self-awareness:** By focusing on each muscle group in the body, progressive relaxation can help to increase self-awareness and promote a deeper sense of body–mind connection.

* **Enhanced immune system function:** Progressive relaxation has been shown to enhance immune system function, which can improve overall health and well-being.

Overall, progressive relaxation is a simple and effective technique that can have numerous benefits for both physical and mental health.

STEPS TO COMPLETE PROGRESSIVE MUSCLE RELAXATION (PMR)

* **Find a comfortable position:** Find a quiet and comfortable place to sit or lie down. Loosen any tight clothing or accessories that may interfere with the relaxation process.

* **Start with deep breathing:** Take a few deep breaths in through your nose and out through your mouth. Focus on breathing deeply into your belly, allowing your abdomen to expand as you inhale and contract as you exhale.

* **Tense and release each muscle group:** Start at your toes and work your way up your body, tensing and then releasing each muscle group in turn. For each muscle group, tense the muscle group for five to ten seconds and then release and relax for ten to twenty seconds. Repeat this process for each muscle group.

* **Focus on the sensations:** As you tense and release each muscle group, focus your attention on the sensations in your body. Pay attention to the feeling of tension as you tense the muscle group and then the feeling of relaxation as you release it.

* **Move up your body:** Continue the process of tensing and releasing each muscle group, moving up your body from your toes to the top of your head. Make sure to include all major muscle groups in the process, including your feet, legs, hips, stomach, chest, arms, shoulders, neck, and face.

* **End with relaxation:** Once you have completed the tensing and releasing of all muscle groups, take a few moments to enjoy the feeling of deep relaxation in your body. Take a few more deep breaths, and let your body and mind remain calm and relaxed.

Remember, PMR is a technique that requires practice, so it may take a few sessions to feel full results. Scan the QR code to watch the video on how to practice PMR:

MUSIC AND MOVEMENT

Music and movement can significantly impact brain relaxation. Music has the ability to impact our emotions. Depending on the rhythm and lyrics of a song, music can make us feel sad, excited, happy, or calm. Moving the body can be calming and help release tension and endorphins in the brain, depending on how fast or slow you move. Here are some ways that they can help.

* **Music can reduce stress:** Listening to calming music can reduce the levels of the stress hormone cortisol in the body, which can help to reduce feelings of anxiety and promote relaxation.

* **Movement can release tension:** Stretching exercises can help release muscle tension and promote relaxation.

* **Music can promote mindfulness:** Listening to music can help to promote mindfulness, which is a state of present-moment aware-ness. This can help to calm the mind and promote relaxation.

* **Movement can increase blood flow:** Physical movement can increase blood flow to the brain, which can help to improve cogni-tive function and reduce stress.

* **Music can induce a meditative state:** Certain types of music, such as ambient or instrumental music, can induce a meditative state in the brain, which can promote relaxation and reduce stress.

* **Movement can improve sleep:** Regular physical activity can help improve sleep quality, which can positively impact overall mental health and well-being.

Overall, both music and movement can have a powerful impact on relaxing the brain and promoting feelings of calm and relaxation. Incorporating these practices into your daily routine can greatly reduce stress and improve overall well-being.

WHITE NOISE

White noise can have a significant impact on relaxing the brain. White noise is a type of sound that contains all frequencies at the same intensity level, creating a soothing, consistent sound that can help to mask other sounds and promote relaxation. Here are some of the key ways that white noise can help to relax the brain:

* **Promotes better sleep:** White noise can help to create a calming environment conducive to sleep. By masking other sounds and creating a consistent background noise, white noise can help to promote deeper, more restful sleep.

* **Reduces stress and anxiety:** White noise can help to reduce stress and anxiety by creating a calming, soothing environment. The consistent white noise can help block out other distracting or anxiety-provoking sounds, promoting relaxation and calmness.

* **Improves focus and concentration:** White noise can also help to improve focus and concentration by reducing distractions and creating a consistent background sound that can help to block out other noises and improve mental clarity.

✳ **Eases symptoms of tinnitus:** Tinnitus is a condition that causes a constant ringing or buzzing sound in the ears. White noise can help to mask the sound of tinnitus and provide relief from the symptoms.

Examples of White Noise

✳ **White noise machines:** Many types of white noise machines are available, ranging from simple devices that generate a basic white noise sound to more advanced machines that can be customized with different sounds and settings.

✳ **Nature sounds:** Many people find that nature sounds, such as the sound of rain, waves, or a babbling brook, can be very relaxing and soothing. These sounds can also be combined with white noise to create a more complex background sound.

✳ **Household appliances:** Some common household appliances, such as fans, air conditioners, and humidifiers, can also generate white noise. These devices can be particularly useful for promoting sleep and relaxation.

✳ **Online white noise generators:** Some websites and apps offer white noise generators that can be customized with different sounds and settings. These generators can be accessed on a computer or mobile device, making them easy to use at home or on the go.

✳ **TV or radio static:** The sound of static from a TV or radio can also be used as a form of white noise. While this type of white noise may not be as soothing as other options, it can still be effective at masking other sounds and promoting relaxation.

Many different types of white noise can be used to promote relaxation and mask other sounds. The best type of white noise will depend on individual preferences and needs. White noise can be a powerful tool for promoting relaxation and reducing stress and anxiety. Whether used for sleep, focus, or general relaxation, white noise can provide a soothing background sound that can help to calm the brain and promote a greater sense of overall well-being.

Scan the following QR code to see a selection of white noise devices.

AROMATHERAPY

Aromatherapy is the use of essential oils and other aromatic compounds to improve physical, emotional, and mental well-being. The practice is based on the belief that certain scents can stimulate the brain to release chemicals that promote relaxation, calmness, and a sense of well-being. (When using aromatherapy, it's important to remember that essential oils are highly concentrated and should be used with caution. Be sure to follow the instructions carefully and consult a trained aromatherapist or health-care provider if you have any questions or concerns.)

BENEFITS OF AROMATHERAPY IN RELAXING THE BRAIN

* **Reduces stress and anxiety:** Certain essential oils like lavender, chamomile, and bergamot have been shown to reduce stress and anxiety by promoting relaxation and calming the mind.

* **Improves sleep:** Aromatherapy can also help to improve sleep quality by promoting relaxation and reducing anxiety. Essential

oils like lavender, valerian, and ylang-ylang have been shown to have a calming effect on the mind and promote sleep.

* **Boosts mood:** Aromatherapy has been shown to positively affect mood and emotional well-being. Essential oils like peppermint, lemon, and frankincense can help to improve mood and reduce feelings of stress and anxiety.

* **Improves cognitive function:** Aromatherapy can also help improve cognitive function by stimulating the brain and increasing alertness and focus. Essential oils like rosemary and peppermint have been shown to improve cognitive function and memory.

* **Relieves headaches:** Certain essential oils like peppermint and lavender have been shown to relieve headaches and migraines by promoting relaxation and reducing tension.

Overall, aromatherapy can be a safe and effective way to promote relaxation and reduce stress and anxiety. It is important to note, however, that essential oils should be used with caution and under the guidance of a trained aromatherapist or healthcare provider. Scan the QR code to see a selection of essential oils and diffusers.

There are many ways to use aromatherapy, depending on your needs and preferences.

COMMON METHODS FOR AROMATHERAPY

* **Inhalation:** This is the most common method of aromatherapy. You can inhale the essential oils directly from the bottle, use a diffuser, or add a few drops to a bowl of hot water and inhale the steam.

* **Massage:** You can add a few drops of essential oil to a carrier oil, such as coconut or jojoba oil, and use it for massage. This method is particularly useful for relieving muscle tension and promoting relaxation.

* **Bath:** Adding a few drops of essential oil to your bathwater creates a relaxing and soothing atmosphere. Be sure to mix the oil with a carrier oil or Epsom salts to help disperse the oil in the water.

* **Topical application:** You can apply diluted essential oils directly to the skin for a variety of purposes, such as relieving headaches or promoting skin health. Be sure to dilute the essential oil with a carrier oil before applying it to the skin.

* **Room spray:** You can make a room spray by adding essential oils to water and spraying it around your home or workspace. This is a great way to create a relaxing atmosphere and promote mental clarity.

Remember that essential oils are highly concentrated and should be used with caution. Be sure to follow the instructions carefully and consult a trained aromatherapist or healthcare provider if you have any questions or concerns.

MASSAGE

Massage can have numerous benefits for the relaxation of the brain. Following are some of the key benefits of massage:

* **Reduces stress and anxiety:** Massage can help to reduce levels of cortisol, the hormone associated with stress, and increase levels of serotonin and dopamine, which can promote feelings of relaxation and happiness.

* **Improves sleep:** Massage can also help improve sleep quality by reducing stress and promoting relaxation. This can benefit the brain, including improving memory and cognitive function.

* **Reduces muscle tension and pain:** Massage can help to release tension in the muscles, which can contribute to headaches, migraines, and other forms of pain. Massage can help to promote relaxation throughout the body, including the brain, by reducing muscle tension and pain.

* **Improves circulation:** Massage can help to improve blood flow and circulation throughout the body, including the brain. This can help to deliver oxygen and nutrients to the brain, supporting brain health and function.

* **Promotes relaxation and calmness:** The gentle, soothing touch of massage can promote relaxation and calmness throughout the body and mind. This can help reduce stress and anxiety and promote greater well-being.

Massage can be a powerful tool for promoting relaxation and reducing stress and anxiety, which can have numerous benefits for the brain and overall health. If you cannot afford to get regular massages at a spa, some gyms offer massage beds as part of their services.

EXERCISE

Exercise can significantly impact brain relaxation. The following are some of the key ways that exercise can help to promote relaxation.

* **Reduces stress and anxiety:** Exercise can help to reduce levels of the stress hormone cortisol and increase levels of endorphins, promoting feelings of happiness and relaxation.

* **Improves sleep:** Regular exercise can help promote better sleep, which has numerous benefits for the brain, including improving memory, cognitive function, and overall well-being.

* **Increases blood flow to the brain:** Exercise can help to increase blood flow to the brain, delivering more oxygen and nutrients to support brain health and function.

* **Boosts mood:** Exercise has been shown to positively impact mood, reducing feelings of depression and anxiety and promoting a greater sense of overall well-being.

* **Promotes mindfulness:** Exercise can also promote mindfulness and a greater sense of presence in the moment, which can help to reduce feelings of stress and promote relaxation.

Overall, exercise can be a powerful tool for promoting relaxation and reducing stress and anxiety. Regular exercise can provide numerous benefits for the brain and overall health, whether it's a brisk walk, a workout class, a gym workout, or dancing.

MEDITATION

Meditation is practiced in many ways. Some people utilize yoga and mantras, which they find relaxing and empowering. However, for most Christians, meditation involves focusing on the words of God written in the Bible, reading books, or listening to podcasts that explore the Word of God in depth, talking to God about their challenges, and believing that He will comfort, provide solutions, and work miracles in their lives. According to research conducted by researchers at Baylor University, people who pray to a loving and protective God are less likely to experience anxiety-related disorders—worry, fear, self-consciousness, social anxiety, and obsessive-compulsive behavior—compared to people who pray but don't really expect to receive any comfort or protection from God. The researchers examined the data of 1,714 volunteers who participated in the most recent Baylor Religion Survey. They focused on general anxiety, social anxiety, obsession, and compulsion.[17]

David spoke about the benefits of meditating on the words of God in the book of Psalms. He highlights the outcome of being intentional about meditating on God's words multiple times a day and choosing to spend time with God rather than doing things that were not spiritually uplifting.

Blessed is the man who walks not in the counsel of the ungodly, nor stands in the path of sinners, nor sits in the seat of the scornful; But his delight is in the law of the Lord, and in His law, he meditates day and night. He shall be like a tree planted by the rivers of water, that brings forth its fruit in its season, whose leaf also shall not wither; And whatever he does shall prosper. (Psalm 1:1–4 NKJV)

Following are some ways in which meditation on the Bible can have an impact on relaxing the brain.

* **Focusing the mind:** Meditation on God's promises or other spiritual texts can help focus the mind on a single point of concentration. By focusing on God's Word, you can let go of distracting thoughts and worries and experience a greater sense of peace and tranquility through the power of God.

* **Reducing stress:** The Bible contains many verses that encourage believers to trust in God and to cast their cares upon Him. Meditating on these verses can help to reduce stress and anxiety and promote a greater sense of calmness.

✳ **Promoting gratitude:** Many verses in the Bible encourage us to give thanks and focus on the blessings in our lives. Meditating on these verses and expressing gratitude can help individuals experience a greater sense of peace and contentment.

Overall, meditation on the Bible can significantly impact brain relaxation and promote spiritual and emotional well-being. By incorporating regular meditation on Bible verses into your spiritual practice, you can experience God's power in your life and enjoy a deeper sense of peace and connection with God.

I hope you find these options for relaxing your brain helpful. You can also combine some of them for optimal results. For example, you could combine deep breathing with progressive muscle relaxation and add white noise and aromatherapy through a diffuser.

Utilize the checklist below to identify the best relaxation techniques or strategies for you. If you have a technique or strategy that you use but is not on this list, please add to the blank spaces below.

☐ Prayer

☐ Deep Breathing

☐ Progressive Muscle Relaxation

☐ White Noise

☐ Aromatherapy

☐ Music and Movement

☐ Massage

☐ Exercise

☐ Meditation

☐ _____

☐ _____

☐ _____

After you have completed your relaxation exercises, your brain should be calmer, and you should experience less tension, more clarity, and feel less overwhelmed. Now, it is time to focus on your stressors and figure out a plan to address each one. This act of facing your problems to gain control and resolution should help reduce your stress signals and symptoms.

In this section, I will highlight strategies for effectively resolving stressors and achieving peace of mind.

CATEGORIZE YOUR STRESSORS

In Chapter 4, you identified your stressors on the checklist provided. It is time to revisit that list to utilize the "categorize your stressors" strategy. Categorizing your stressors can be very effective because it helps you identify things that are in your control and the things you spend hours worrying about that you cannot control. Whenever I share this strategy with my clients, they are usually amazed at how many of their stressors are outside of their control. They usually express how much lighter and liberated they feel after identifying the things they no longer need to worry about.

Picture yourself walking with ten blocks in a bag on your back; you are feeling tired, weak, and in pain. Then you decide to start taking some of the blocks out, and instantly, you start to feel lighter and more hopeful about carrying what is left. Some people, however, may refuse to take out the blocks they don't control because they may experience anxiety associated with letting go.

The truth is that worrying about things you cannot change does not change the outcome of the situation; however, it changes you. It causes you to feel stressed, and as we have been learning, exposure to long-term stress leads to chronic stress and eventually impacts your health. So, holding on to things you cannot change eventually hurts you.

Some challenges are very difficult to live with or experience; not having control over them does not diminish their impact on us physically and emotionally. The following steps will help you categorize your stressors and develop coping skills to help you through your challenges.

STEP 1

The first step in categorizing your stressors is to identify all your stressors. If you have not completed this activity previously, please use Appendix III to write down all your stressors. It does not matter how long your list becomes; leave no stressor out.

STEP 2

Utilize Appendix V to place each stressor under the two categories: "What is in your control" and "What is not in your control." Remember that all the stressors that you cannot change, regardless of how much you think about them, should be placed under "What is not in your control." All the stressors you can change and plan for should be placed under "What you can control."

MANAGING YOUR STRESSORS

Things I Cannot Control

Let's address managing the stressors you cannot control. The stressors you placed under this category are things that you cannot change or have attempted to change but realized that your efforts have not produced the desired results. Accepting this loss of control can be difficult and cause a lot of anxiety. If you begin to feel anxious, try to utilize your relaxation strategies to calm down and relax. For the stressors you cannot control, you let them go. Letting go can be a physical walking away or a decision you make. You might be in a toxic work environment or relationship and have tried to create change; however, change does not happen. You may choose to walk away, or you may choose to accept that you cannot change the people or situations and work on controlling your thoughts to not think about it or worry about it.

Self-talk is critical, every time a thought related to the stressors pops into your mind, you should say to yourself, "I am choosing not to think about this because I realize that I have no power to change it." The reality is that thoughts are very intrusive, and you may have to practice this self-talk activity for a little while until you have trained your brain. You see, our brains can be trained to do almost anything once we repeat them consistently—just like driving. Repeat to yourself your new decision to "let go" whenever that stressor comes into your mind. Your brain will create a pathway for it, eventually resolving it on its own. Isn't the brain amazing? We are truly wonderfully created.

When we let things go that are outside of our control, we can give them to God, who controls everything. Sometimes, we forget that we have a God who is all-powerful and can take care of all our concerns and worries. He promised that He would handle all our problems if we let Him. Letting go is creating opportunities for us to experience God's supernatural peace and amazing miracles in our lives. When God works out the issues we cannot control, it forces us to see His power and the revelation of the God factor in our lives. So, be at peace about letting go because God's got this! Whenever you feel anxious about your stressors, repeat to yourself, "God's got this!"

Paul wrote in the book of Hebrews 11:1 (NLT), "Faith shows the reality of what we hope for; it is the evidence of things we cannot see." The unknown can feel scary; however, when we trust God and have faith that He will keep His promises, we can let go and have sweet peace. So, letting go is not giving up; it's giving God a chance to take control of our situations.

Luke shares one of the most powerful messages from Jesus to us about the importance of believing and trusting in His power to change our circumstances, in Luke 12:25–31 (NLT).

"Can all your worries add a single moment to your life? And if worry can't accomplish a little thing like that, what's the use of worrying over bigger things? Look at the lilies and how they grow. They don't work or make their clothing, yet Solomon, in all his glory, was not dressed as beautifully as they are. And if God cares so wonderfully for flowers that are here today and thrown into the fire tomorrow, he will certainly care for you. Why do you have so little faith? And don't be concerned about what to eat and what to drink. Don't worry about such things. These things dominate the thoughts of unbelievers all over the world, but your Father already knows your needs. Seek the Kingdom of God above all else, and he will give you everything you need."

Amen! {Drop the mic!}

Things I Can Control

Let's address the stressors you can control. The stressors you placed in this category are things you can change. Things you can control are things that you can contemplate a strategy for and implement the strategy to create change. These things depend on the choices you make or do not make. So, you must have a plan for the things you can control. Take each stressor individually and create a thorough plan. Utilize Appendix VI to write down your stressor and your plan. When we leave things hanging, it can cause us to become anxious and worry because we are unsure of the next steps. Having a plan helps significantly reduce your stress because you clearly know your next steps. I am using the word *reduce* your stress because I am aware that once you have a plan, then a whole new set of worries manifest because of fears about whether or not the plan will work, which is the unknown factor and the execution of your plan. I will address the issues of fear and execution later.

Addressing multiple stressors can be overwhelming, especially if some are complex. If you are struggling with creating a plan for any of your stressors, seek support from a specialist in the area. For matters of the heart, seek a trained, licensed therapist; for other areas, seek a specialist. For example, if you are struggling with financial challenges and unsure of the way forward, talk with a financial advisor; if you are struggling with mental health challenges, marriage, or parenting, talk with a trained mental health therapist. What I am saying is that you don't have to lose sleep and worry about a problem you do not have the capacity to address on your own; seek help.

PRIORITIZE

Another helpful strategy for planning for the stressors you can control is the skill of prioritizing. Prioritizing is identifying the most important stressors and parking the ones that are least important in the parking lot. A car should legally have four passengers based on the number of seatbelts for safety. Any extra people and it becomes crowded, cramped, and unsafe. You have to decide to take one set of passengers in your car to their destination and return to get the others.

Processing too many issues in your brain can cause brain overcrowding and overload, which can result in your experiencing chronic stress. Therefore, prioritizing your stressors can be very helpful in reducing stress because it allows you to focus on the most important areas first. When you focus on the most important areas in a manageable way, then you will have the capacity to think clearly and create and execute your plan more quickly and efficiently.

Scan the QR code to watch a video
on prioritizing and scheduling away stress.

TRUST GOD WITH YOUR PLANS

Having plans is great; however, sometimes, we fail to execute our plans because of the fear of failure. Many plans die out and are never realized because of fear. Thinking of the unknown naturally produces feelings of fear because you truly don't know the outcome. The key is not to allow that fear to make you stop; instead, push through it.

Having the God factor is the perfect remedy for the fear factor. Fear is the complete opposite of faith. Fear is rooted in the discomfort and uncertainty of the unknown, while faith, on the other hand, requires us to trust in what we cannot see. Hebrews 11:1 (NKJV) says, "Now faith is the substance of things hoped for, the evidence of things not seen." Faith and fear cannot exist in the same space. Whatever plans we have, God has promised that if we consult Him about our plans, He will give us advice and bring our vision to reality. That sounds like a great deal to me. The God who created the universe, the God who just spoke and things came into being, is offering to execute whatever plans you have; in the grand scheme of things, our problems seem so minute for a big God.

I faced so many fearful thoughts and feelings that translated into avoidance and self-sabotaging when God impressed on me to write this book. I was hyper-focused on all the things that could go wrong and was convincing myself that it would not work. I realized quickly that I needed the God factor. I needed to pray and ask God to strengthen me and show me the way forward. I chose to believe Him; I chose faith. So the fact that you are reading this book is a testament that God keeps His promises.

Look at the Bible verses below that reveal God's interest in your plans and His assurance to guide you and lead you to a life of blessings and prosperity.

GOD'S PROMISES FOR YOUR PLANS

* **Jeremiah 29:11** (NIV)
  "For I know the plans I have for you," declares the Lord, "plans to prosper you and not to harm you, plans to give you hope and a future."

* **Proverbs 3:5–6** (NLT)
  "Trust in the Lord with all your heart; do not depend on your own understanding. Seek His will in all you do, and he will show you which path to take."

* **Proverbs 16:3** (NIV)

  "Commit to the Lord whatever you do, and he will establish your plans."

* **Proverbs 16:9** (NIV)

  "In their hearts, humans plan their course, but the Lord establishes their steps."

* **Proverbs 15:22** (NKJV)

  "Without counsel, plans go awry. But in the multitude of counselors, they are established."

* **Proverbs 19:21** (NLT)

  "You can make many plans, but the Lord's purpose will prevail."

* **Deuteronomy 31:8** (NIV)

  "The Lord himself goes before you and will be with you; he will never leave or forsake you. Do not be afraid; do not be discouraged."

This is my prayer for you: "May He grant your heart's desires and make all your plans succeed." (Psalm 20:4 NLT).

HAVE A POSITIVE MINDSET/GRATITUDE

Darkness cannot drive out darkness: only light can do that.
Hate cannot drive out hate: only love can do that.
– Martin Luther King, Jr.

Keep your face always toward the sunshine—
and shadows will fall behind you.

– Walt Whitman

A positive mindset is an attitude or mental state that focuses on the positive aspects of life and situations rather than dwelling on negative or challenging circumstances. It involves cultivating hope and optimism, even in the face of adversity.

Having a positive mindset means:

- ✓ Being able to reframe challenges as opportunities for growth and learning.
- ✓ Seeing setbacks as temporary rather than permanent.
- ✓ Being grateful for what you have, rather than focusing on what you lack—contentment.
- ✓ Looking for the good in yourself and others.

People with a positive mindset tend to have better mental and physical health, stronger relationships, and more success in their personal and professional lives. They approach problems with creativity and resilience and can often bounce back from setbacks more quickly.

A growing body of research highlights the benefits of positive thoughts and emotions. Following are some examples of research findings.

- ✳ **Increased well-being:** A study by Lyubomirsky, S., Dickerhoof, R., Boehm, J. K., & Sheldon, K.M. 2011 found that individuals who were motivated to engage in intentional activities such as gratitude and optimism to cultivate positive emotions experienced increases in their overall sense of well-being.[18]

- ✳ **Improved resilience:** Research by Cohn, M. A., Fredrickson, B. L., Brown, S. L., Mikels, J. A., & Conway, A. M. (2009) found that individuals who experienced positive emotions were better able to bounce back from stressful situations and cope with adversity.[19]

- ✳ **Better physical health:** [20]A study found that habitual positive emotions and positive social connections had a positive effect on individuals' physical health measured by their vagal to. According to the article, the findings suggested that habitually experiencing positive emotions may be an essential psychological nutrient for autonomic health.[21]

✳ **Improved cognitive function:** Research by Fredrickson and Branigan (2005) found that individuals who experienced positive emotions were better able to solve problems and engage in creative thinking than those who experienced negative emotions.[22]

✳ **Social Connections:** A study conducted by Bethany E. Kok and her colleagues revealed that individuals who experience positive emotions tend to perceive themselves as more socially connected. The study found that people's positive perception of their social connections with others has a positive impact on their emotional well-being and physical health, as measured by their vagal tone.[23].

Overall, these studies suggest that cultivating positive thoughts and emotions can have numerous benefits for our mental and physical health, as well as our social relationships and cognitive function.

Thoughts are intrusive, which means they come into our minds when we least expect them. Sometimes , they're happy, and sometimes, there are thoughts about unpleasant experiences or worries that we might have. What we think affects how we feel and what we do. Negative thoughts don't just come into our minds and do nothing; they impact us and our lives. When thoughts are not pleasant, they bring unpleasant feelings. If not addressed, we eventually do unhealthy things like not eating, not sleeping, isolating ourselves, or being unkind to people. Consequently, there are benefits to your health and well-being if you intentionally control negative thoughts to reduce or eliminate them.

HOW TO CONTROL NEGATIVE THOUGHTS

In the Bible, several passages address the power of negative thoughts; I will reference a few. Mathew wrote in Matthew 15:19 (NLT), "For from the heart come evil thoughts, murder, adultery, all sexual immorality, theft, lying, and slander." This verse emphasizes that our thoughts impact our behaviors and focuses on the outcome of evil thoughts. In Proverbs 4:23 (NKJV), Solomon wrote, "Keep your heart with all diligence, for out of it *spring* the issues of life." This verse emphasizes the importance of controlling your thoughts because your thoughts determine your life. What we think can become a reality; what we think becomes who we are as individuals. Negative thoughts can harm us and others if they are not addressed.

The following are three steps to help you control negative thoughts.

STEP 1: EXAMINE YOUR THOUGHTS

To examine means to inspect or scrutinize something carefully and thoroughly to evaluate, understand, or determine its characteristics, qualities, or condition. It involves a systematic and detailed analysis of the object of the examination in order to gain knowledge or understanding about it. Remember the phrase I used earlier: "We cannot fix what we do not understand." So, the first step to controlling our thoughts is to understand the nature of our thoughts.

* **Become aware of your thoughts:** Pay attention to your thoughts as they occur, without judging or analyzing them. Try to observe them objectively, as if you were an outside observer. If you observe a change in your mood, then pause and explore whether or not a thought was connected to your mood change. Sometimes you may notice a change in your mood more readily than your thoughts. Therefore, it is important to reflect on the origin of your change of mood if it is significant or noticeable.

* **Identify patterns:** Look for patterns or themes in your thoughts. Are they mostly positive or negative? Do they tend to focus on certain topics or situations? If you have recurring thoughts, you can write them down to help you identify their patterns and nature. Identifying patterns can help you to understand your mental habits and tendencies.

❋ **Evaluate the accuracy of your thoughts:** Question the accuracy and validity of your thoughts. Are they based on facts or assumptions? Are they logical or irrational? Challenging the accuracy of your thoughts can help you to develop a more realistic and balanced perspective.

❋ **Examine the underlying beliefs:** Explore the underlying beliefs or assumptions that may be driving your thoughts. Are they helpful or harmful? Are they based on past experiences or cultural conditioning? Examining your beliefs can help you to understand and change your thought patterns.

Examining your thoughts requires noticing, focusing on, and processing your thoughts. Some people may not have that ability because their thoughts move rapidly and are sometimes uncontrollable. "Racing thoughts" is a term used to describe a mental state characterized by a rapid, continuous, and often uncontrollable flow of thoughts. People with racing thoughts may experience a constant stream of thoughts that jump from one topic to another without any apparent connection, making it difficult to focus on a particular task or to relax. These thoughts can be overwhelming, intrusive, and distracting and may interfere with daily activities, such as work or social interactions.

Racing thoughts can be a symptom of various mental illness conditions, such as anxiety disorders, bipolar disorder, attention deficit hyperactivity disorder (ADHD), or substance abuse. It can also be a side effect of certain medications or a result of sleep deprivation or stress. Getting professional help from a medical doctor, psychiatrist, and /or licensed therapist is important if you struggle with racing thoughts.

STEP 2: RESOLVE NEGATIVE THOUGHTS

"Resolve" can have multiple meanings depending on the context, but generally, it refers to the act of solving or settling a problem or conflict. It involves making a firm decision or commitment to take action or to bring about a specific outcome or result. "Resolve" can also refer to the determination or perseverance needed to overcome obstacles or achieve a goal. It may involve finding a solution to a difficult situation, resolving a disagreement or dispute, making a decision, or taking action to move forward in a positive direction. Resolving an issue typically involves identifying the problem or challenge, exploring possible solutions or strategies, making a decision or taking action, and evaluating the outcome to determine if it was successful or if further steps are needed.

In this context, "resolve" means addressing and finding a solution to recurring negative thoughts that may be affecting you internally or externally. For instance, if you often think, "I will never pass my chemistry exam," this thought might cause anxiety and hinder your exam performance. After evaluating this thought, you might reach one of two conclusions:

Option A: If you find that your thought is based on evidence—such as never having studied chemistry—then your resolution would be, "My thought is accurate; I need to start studying to improve my chances of passing the exam."

Option B: If your examination of the evidence reveals that you have been studying and consistently scoring between 90 and 100 percent on practice tests, then your resolution would be, "My thought is not accurate; I am prepared to succeed on the exam because I have studied and performed well in practice."

By resolving your thoughts in this way, you can address and mitigate their impact on your performance.

If you allowed that thought to recur without examining and resolving, it would probably negatively impact your ability to achieve your goals and your overall well-being. Sometimes finding a resolution may involve seeking the support of a trained expert in the area you are struggling in. Sometimes your negative thoughts may be rooted in past trauma and pain, and a resolution may require you to engage in therapy to find your healing and resolve that area of your life. So, your thoughts are the window to areas of your life that are doing well and also areas that need improvement and restoration.

STEP 3: USE YOUR RESOLUTION TO CHALLENGE YOUR NEGATIVE THOUGHTS

You may have noticed that some thoughts are recurring and seem to make a comeback even after you have made efforts to distract yourself, ignore them, or resolve them. Interestingly, if the thoughts are positive, they do not seem to be so persistent; however, the negative thoughts for some people seem to come quickly and often. Remember that you cannot control when a thought might pop into your mind sometimes; however, once it's there, you have the opportunity to challenge it with your resolution. Utilizing self-talk, you remind yourself of what you decided to do to address the issue or the memory and repeat that resolution to yourself. You will soon realize that the need to repeat your resolution will be less than before or not needed at all.

So, if we continue with the example above, although you decided that you are going to (A) study to improve your chances of passing your chemistry or (B) not worry about failing because you have been studying, the thought of failing might reoccur. Once this happens, then you repeat your resolution every time that thought pops into your head.

Often, we entertain negative thoughts as if inviting them to sit at our table and engage in conversation. We might think things like, "This might happen, and if it does, it will be horrible and disastrous." We dwell on words like "suppose," "maybe," and "what if," and before we realize it, we're overwhelmed with anxiety, distress, and depression. Instead of letting these negative thoughts disrupt your peace, challenge them. Don't let them take control and undermine your well-being.

Use positive self-talk to reinforce optimism in your life. After you've examined your thoughts and found solutions to your issues or memories, repeat your resolutions to yourself. This practice can be an effective strategy for calming an anxious or worried mind.

STEP 4: PRAY

Prayer is a powerful avenue to combat negative thoughts. There is power in the Word of God. When the devil attempts to use your fears and your past against you, call on God! Hebrews 4:12 (NKJV) says, "For the word of God *is* living and powerful, and sharper than any two-edged sword, piercing even to the division of soul and spirit, and of joints and marrow, and is a discerner of the thoughts and intents of the heart."

This verse highlights the dynamic and transformative power of the Word of God. The verse uses metaphorical language to describe the potency of God's Word. The comparison of the Word of God to a "two-edged sword" emphasizes its ability to penetrate deep into the human soul and divide it into its most essential components, such as thoughts and intentions.

The verse also highlights that the Word of God is "living," indicating that it has a dynamic quality that makes it relevant and applicable to every generation and every problem. It is a source of life and power that can bring about significant changes in your life. God has the power to transform your thoughts.

Talk to God about your recurring negative thoughts and ask Him to give you victory over them, to give you peace of mind and joy unimaginable. In conclusion, after you have examined and resolved your thoughts, challenge your negative thoughts through the power of prayer.

CLEAR YOUR HEAD BEFORE BED (ACTIVITY)

This activity can be very effective in helping you to clear your mind before you sleep and increase self-validation. Clearing your mind and validating yourself before you sleep can reduce anxiety, increase a positive mindset, and improve your sleep.

Complete the phrases below 30 minutes before bedtime nightly. Appendix VII

Today I am grateful and happy that I accomplished:

_____

_____

_____

_____

Tomorrow I will prioritize:

_____

_____

_____

_____

Tomorrow I will do these things if I have extra time:

_____

_____

_____

_____

CHAPTER 6

E – EDUCATE:
PART 2 – BENEFITS OF A HEALTHY AND BALANCED LIFE ON REDUCING STRESS

YOU MAY NOT HAVE THOUGHT OF HOW YOUR LIFESTYLE impacts your stress levels. Many of us just live the best way we know without ever exploring how the choices we make daily—what we do, what we eat, and how we think or whom we associate with, impacts how we manage stress. You are not alone; I only began to explore these areas in depth when I started to experience issues with my health. A health scare has that power, doesn't it? It forces you to stop and think about the brevity of life, and you may become compelled to assess and find solutions to regain your functioning and quality of life. In this chapter, I will share how healthy lifestyle choices and maintaining balance can positively impact our ability to manage stress and experience wellness and happiness.

NUTRITION

Let's start with what we eat—nutrition. Nutrition is the science of how food affects the body and encompasses all the processes involved in the consumption, digestion, absorption, metabolism, and excretion of nutrients found in food. It includes the study of nutrients, such as carbohydrates, proteins, fats, vitamins, and minerals, and how they function in the body.

What we eat can impact our mood, energy levels, and our overall health. Not having a healthy lifestyle can cause us to have health problems which can become stressors in our lives. Consequently, when we are not healthy, it impacts how we manage the stressors in our lives. Therefore, poor nutrition can have a cyclical effect. According to an article published by the Harvard School of Public Health, a balanced diet can support a healthy immune system and the repair of damaged cells. It provides the extra energy needed to cope with stressful events. Early research suggests that certain foods like polyunsaturated fats such as nuts, including omega-3 fats and vegetables, may help to regulate cortisol levels.[24]

The article referenced above also highlighted how chronic stress can impact our eating patterns in the following ways:

* Elevate cortisol levels, which may cause an increase in craving for comforting foods, such as highly processed snacks or sweets, which are high in fat and calories but low in nutrients; it also lowers levels of the hormone leptin (which promotes feeling full) while increasing the hormone ghrelin (that increases appetite).

* Increase in the use of stimulants such as caffeine, energy drinks, and high-calorie snack foods because of fatigue caused by sleep disruption due to stress. Based on research, there is an association between sleep restriction and an increase in cortisol levels.

* Lack of time or motivation to prepare meals that are balanced and healthy.

Overall, nutrition is an essential component of overall health and well-being and is critical for maintaining a healthy body, preventing chronic diseases, and supporting optimal physical and mental performance.[25]

FOODS THAT NEGATIVELY IMPACT OUR HEALTH

* **Processed and junk foods:** Processed and junk foods are often high in added sugars, unhealthy fats, and sodium and low in nutrients. Consuming these foods regularly can contribute to weight gain, inflammation, and chronic diseases such as type 2 diabetes, heart disease, and certain types of cancer.

* **Sugary drinks:** Sugary drinks such as soda, fruit juices, and energy drinks can contribute to weight gain, increase the risk of type 2 diabetes and heart disease, and cause spikes and crashes in blood sugar levels, leading to mood swings and fatigue.

* **Trans fats:** Trans fats are commonly found in processed foods and are known to increase the risk of heart disease, inflammation, and weight gain.

* **Alcohol:** Alcohol can negatively impact mood and disrupt sleep, leading to fatigue and irritability. Excessive alcohol consumption can also lead to liver damage and an increased risk of certain types of cancer.

* **Caffeine:** While caffeine can provide a temporary energy boost, consuming too much caffeine can cause jitters and anxiety and disrupt sleep, leading to fatigue and mood swings.

* **High-sodium foods:** Consuming high amounts of sodium, which is commonly found in processed foods and fast foods, can contribute to high blood pressure and an increased risk of heart disease.

Following are a few ways that nutrition can positively impact stress management:

* **Blood sugar regulation:** Eating a balanced diet with foods with a low glycemic index can help regulate blood sugar levels, preventing spikes and crashes in energy levels that can contribute to stress and anxiety.

✳ **Micronutrient intake:** Micronutrients like vitamins and minerals are essential for the proper functioning of our bodies, including our brain and nervous systems. Consuming a varied diet rich in fruits, vegetables, whole grains, and lean protein sources can help to ensure adequate micronutrient intake, positively impacting our mood and stress levels.

✳ **Gut health:** The gut–brain axis is a bidirectional communication system between the gut and the brain, and a healthy gut microbiome has been shown to positively impact mood and stress levels. The gut microbiome is a community of microorganisms including fungi and bacteria that play a crucial role in digestion and nutrient absorption. Eating a fiber-rich diet, fermented foods, and probiotics can promote a healthy gut microbiome.

✳ **Omega-3 fatty acids:** Omega-3 fatty acids found in fatty fish, flax seeds, and walnuts have been shown to have anti-inflammatory properties and may help to reduce symptoms of anxiety and depression.

Overall, consuming a balanced, varied diet that is rich in whole foods and limiting the intake of processed and sugary foods can positively impact stress management. When we are stressed, it can impact our preparing and choosing nutritious meals; on the other hand, eating nutritious meals can help us to have more stability in our moods and better health, reducing our stressors.

SLEEP

According to the Centers For Disease Control (CDC), one in three adults do not get enough sleep.[26] How much sleep do we need to be healthy? How does sleep impact our ability to manage stress?

The Center for Disease Control recommends the amount of sleep a person should get based on their age.[27] See the following chart.

Sleep requirements by age	
Age	**Hours of sleep needed**
0–3 months	14–17
4–11 months	12–16
1–2 years old	11–14
3–5 years old	10–13
6–12 years old	9–12
13–18 years old	8–10
18–64 years old	7–9
65+	7–8

Getting adequate sleep has not been easy for a lot of people, because of the increasing demands of life within the same twenty-four hours. As a result, we tend to borrow our sleep time to keep up and survive. Sometimes we forfeit sleep to have a good time; me time; binge TV time; or work time. However, not getting adequate sleep hurts our health and well-being. Chronic stress can impact our sleep patterns, and our poor sleep patterns can eventually elevate our chronic stress symptoms. Poor sleep habits or hygiene can impact our health negatively, which can cause stress, and then we also have a cyclical effect.

Let's review some of the negative effects of poor sleep hygiene on our bodies and stress levels.

* **Disrupted Circadian Rhythm:** Poor sleep hygiene can disrupt the body's natural circadian rhythm, which regulates sleep and wake cycles. This disruption can lead to difficulty falling asleep or staying asleep, resulting in sleep deprivation. When the body does not get enough restful sleep, it can exacerbate chronic stress by increasing feelings of anxiety, irritability, and mood swings.

* **Increased cortisol levels:** Poor sleep hygiene can lead to increased levels of cortisol, a stress hormone that the body produces in response to stress. When cortisol levels remain elevated for an extended period, it can lead to chronic stress. Additionally, increased cortisol levels can contribute to weight gain, decreased immune function, and other health problems.

* **Impaired cognitive function:** Poor sleep hygiene can impair cognitive function, including memory, attention, and decision-making skills. When these cognitive functions are compromised, it can make it more challenging to cope with stressors, leading to chronic stress.

* **Physical health problems:** Poor sleep hygiene can lead to a range of physical health problems, including obesity, diabetes, cardiovascular disease, and chronic pain. These health problems can add to the burden of chronic stress, leading to a vicious cycle of poor sleep and ongoing stress.

Did You Know?

Sleep is a critical factor in melatonin production because melatonin is primarily produced during the night while we sleep. Studies have shown that melatonin production increases during the first few hours of sleep and then declines as we approach morning.

Low melatonin levels can impact serotonin production in several ways, including by regulating the activity of the enzymes involved in serotonin synthesis, and by disrupting sleep patterns. Therefore, maintaining healthy melatonin levels is crucial for regulating serotonin levels and promoting overall mental and physical well-being. Serotonin is primarily produced in the gut and brainstem and is involved in regulating mood, appetite, and sleep. Specifically, melatonin can increase the activity of the enzyme tryptophan hydroxylase, which is necessary for serotonin production. This suggests that low melatonin levels may lead to decreased serotonin production, which could contribute to mood disorders.

GOOD SLEEP HYGIENE

Good sleep hygiene can have several benefits in managing chronic stress. Following are some of the benefits of good sleep hygiene on chronic stress.

* **Improves mood:** Good sleep hygiene can help to regulate the production of serotonin, a neurotransmitter that is involved in regulating mood. Getting adequate, restful sleep can help to reduce feelings of anxiety and irritability, improving overall mood and well-being.

* **Boosts cognitive function:** Good sleep hygiene can enhance cognitive function, including memory, attention, and decision-making skills. When these cognitive functions are optimized, it can make it easier to cope with stressors and manage chronic stress.

* **Reduces cortisol levels:** Good sleep hygiene can help to regulate the production of cortisol, a stress hormone that the body produces in response to stress. Getting adequate sleep can help to lower cortisol levels, reducing the burden of chronic stress on the body.

* **Enhances immune function:** Good sleep hygiene can enhance immune function, helping the body better cope with stressors and reducing the risk of illness. Chronic stress can impair immune function, making it more challenging for the body to fight off infections and other health problems.

✳ **Promotes physical health:** Good sleep hygiene is essential for promoting physical health, including cardiovascular health, weight management, and reducing the risk of chronic diseases such as diabetes and hypertension. When physical health is optimized, it can help to reduce the burden of chronic stress on the body.

In summary, good sleep hygiene can have several benefits in managing chronic stress, including improving mood, boosting cognitive function, reducing cortisol levels, enhancing immune function, and promoting physical health. To optimize these benefits, it is essential to establish healthy sleep habits, such as setting a consistent sleep schedule, creating a relaxing sleep environment, and avoiding electronic devices before bedtime.

EXERCISE

The benefits of exercise are numerous for both physical and mental health. Exercise improves cardiovascular health by strengthening the heart muscle and reducing the risk of heart disease. It helps with weight management and boosts the immune system, reducing the risk of infections and illness. It reduces the risk of chronic diseases, lowering the risk of developing chronic diseases such as type 2 diabetes, high blood pressure, and certain types of cancer. Exercise also helps to reduce symptoms of anxiety and depression, improve mood, and enhance cognitive function. It increases energy levels, improves sleep quality, improves bone density, and reduces the risk of osteoporosis. I am not done yet; exercise improves flexibility and balance.

You may notice, like I did, that exercise impacts every organ in our bodies. It would seem that if we are not engaging in exercise, we are in trouble of not having a healthy life. Exercise enhances the overall quality of life and can help us to feel better physically and mentally, leading to an improved quality of life.

Did You Know?

Did you know that the lymph system requires **breathing** and **movement** from the body's muscles to help move fluids and remove waste from the body?

The pooling of lymphatic fluids can lead to blockages and swelling, known as *lymphatic edema*. This occurs through the accumulation of toxins, reducing the function of cells and potentially leading to metabolic and infectious complications. **Completing 10,000 steps** daily or exercising for at least thirty minutes provides continuous physiological movement. The resulting skeletal muscle contractions compress the lymphatic vessels and open the one-way valves, encouraging fluid-containing waste and toxins to be removed.

And to think that I thought exercise was optional! It is necessary for our health and well-being. Regular exercise seems to help keep us healthy and reduce possible stressors. On the other hand, it can help improve your health and reduce your stress if you are struggling with chronic stress.

Exercise can be a highly effective stress management tool, and incorporating regular physical activity into your routine can significantly impact your overall health and well-being.

BALANCE

The word "balance" can have different meanings depending on the context in which it is used. For example, balance refers to the ability to maintain a stable and upright position, either when standing still or moving; financial balance refers to having enough income or resources to cover one's expenses and maintain a stable financial situation. More broadly, balance often implies a state of equilibrium, where various elements are in harmony and not overly dominant or deficient, leading to a healthy and stable situation.

We live in a fast-paced world filled with daily routines, hectic schedules, multiple relationships that need nurturing, and the need to take care of ourselves. It's a lot, and can become overwhelming and sometimes feel frustrating. It's hard to juggle our needs, the needs of work, and the needs of the relationships in our lives. Just thinking about achieving balance can produce great anxiety for many people, because of not knowing how to manage it all. Sometimes you may succeed in one area or a few areas, and it feels great; however, this is momentary because other areas in your life might be falling apart. It makes you wonder if it is possible to achieve balance at all.

I want to encourage you today by letting you know that balance is possible. However, it requires a lot of intentionality and sacrifice to achieve it.

Imagine a board placed on an axle in the center, and two identical weights are placed at either end of the board. The board will be perfectly balanced because the weights on each side are equal and opposite.

Now, imagine moving one of the weights closer to the center of the board. This will cause the board to tip toward the heavier weight, disrupting the balance. As a result, the weight on that side will be reduced, and the weight on the other side will become heavier.

On the other hand, if you move the weight toward the outer edge of the board, the weight on that side will increase, and the weight on the other side will decrease. Again, this will cause the board to tip toward the heavier weight, disrupting the balance.

Therefore, being in the middle on a board on an axle is necessary to create balance because it ensures that the weights on each side are equal and opposite. Any deviation from the center will result in an imbalance, and the board will tip toward the heavier weight.

If we indulge too heavily in any area of our lives, it detracts from other areas. These deficits can cause us to experience stress in our relationships, work, health, and mind. Let's look at some scenarios. What happens to your family if you spend too much time with friends? What happens to your work if you spend too much time with your family? What happens to your health if you spend too much time working? The key here is having an extremely good understanding of your needs for the most important areas of your life and then finding the balance. There are times when things will be off-balance; however, it should not be for long periods.

Living an unbalanced life can negatively impact an individual's physical, emotional, and mental well-being. Following are a few examples.

* **Stress and burnout:** When people focus too much on one area of their lives, such as work, they may experience chronic stress, leading to burnout. Overworking and neglecting other areas of life can cause fatigue, reduced productivity, and a sense of disengagement from life.

* **Poor physical health:** Lack of balance in lifestyle can lead to poor physical health, such as poor sleep quality, poor diet, and lack of physical activity. Over time, this can increase the risk of chronic diseases such as obesity, diabetes, hypertension, and heart disease.

* **Strained relationships:** An unbalanced life can lead to neglecting relationships, causing a strain on them. Unbalanced individuals can fail to keep up with their friends, family, and loved ones, causing them to feel neglected or unimportant.

* **Negative emotional health:** Living an unbalanced life can negatively impact one's emotional well-being, causing a range of negative emotions, such as anxiety, depression, and feelings of isolation or loneliness.

* **Decreased overall satisfaction with life:** An unbalanced life may lead to dissatisfaction and disappointment, despite achieving success in one area.

Overall, an unbalanced life can lead to a lack of fulfillment and a general sense of unhappiness. Therefore, one of the keys to a happy life is balance. Having balance debunks the concept that "we can have it all." The concept of "having it all" implies that we can achieve success in all areas of our lives simultaneously without making any trade-offs or sacrifices. However, the idea of having balance suggests that we are not overexerting ourselves in any area but spreading our time between the things we prioritize. We must make conscious choices and prioritize certain areas of our lives over others.

For example, suppose we want to have a successful career. In that case, we may need to prioritize our work over other areas of our lives, such as family, hobbies, or personal relationships. Alternatively, we may need to make career sacrifices or forego certain opportunities if we want to prioritize our relationships.

The idea of balance recognizes that our resources, including time, energy, and attention, are finite and limited. Therefore, we must intentionally allocate and share these resources to achieve balance in our lives. This may mean that we cannot have everything we want all at once, but rather, we must make choices and prioritize what is most important to us in the present moment.

It is not possible to achieve all we want from work, all we want from our relationships, and all we want from self-care without giving up on some things for a while. It can become challenging when we want to have it all at once. To achieve balance, we have to say no to people and things to make room for the important things and people in our lives at that moment in time. When you balance work, family, spirituality, and personal activities, you are less likely to feel overwhelmed and stressed.

Leading a balanced life can have numerous benefits for physical, mental, and emotional health. The following are some of the key benefits.

* **Improved physical health:** A balanced life can lead to better physical health. When you prioritize exercise, healthy eating, and sleep, you are more likely to have a strong immune system, lower blood pressure, and reduced risk of chronic diseases.

* **Increased happiness:** When you have a balanced life, you are more likely to feel fulfilled and satisfied with your life. This can lead to greater happiness and well-being.

* **Better relationships:** When you balance work and personal life, you have more time to spend with family and friends. This can improve your relationships and strengthen your social connections.

* **Increased productivity:** When you prioritize your time and have a balance between work and personal life, you are more likely to be productive and focused when you are working.

* **Improved mental health:** A balanced life can also lead to better mental health. When you have time for relaxation and self-care, you are less likely to experience burnout, anxiety, and depression.

* **Greater sense of purpose:** When you balance work, family, and personal activities, you are more likely to have a sense of purpose and direction in your life.

Balance is not something you find; it's something you create

– Jana Kingsford.

Ending this chapter on the topic of balance is intentional because it flows very well into the next chapter that explores A – Adjust in the R.E.A.L. Stress Management Approach. Creating a balanced life requires adjusting, being open to change, and having flexibility. However, I am well aware that it is easier said than done. I want to remind you that God is with you. One of my all-time favorite texts is found in Isaiah 41:10 (NLT), which says: "Don't be afraid, for I am with you. Don't be discouraged, for I am your God. I will strengthen you and help you. I will hold you up with my victorious right hand."

Isaiah was a prophet in ancient Israel who lived during political turmoil and uncertainty. When God gave him this text, Isaiah was likely experiencing fear and discouragement due to the difficult circumstances around him.

The text is a message of comfort and reassurance from God to Isaiah. God tells Isaiah not to be afraid or discouraged because He is with him and will help him. Further in the text, God offers to strengthen Isaiah and help him. He also promises him victory through His power.

This message applies to us: "Jesus Christ is the same yesterday, today, and forever" (Hebrews 13:8 NLT). When faced with challenges that cause us to be fearful and feel hopeless, He promises to comfort, strengthen, help, and deliver us out of difficulty. Such beautiful, reassuring promises! When we utilize the God factor, we tap into divine resources.

As you venture into making life-changing adjustments, it can feel overwhelming and have the potential to make you weak in your knees and cause you to lose sleep. I want to encourage you to ask God for help or—I should say—accept His help because His right hand is already extended to you. Try to create an image of God extending His hand to you and hold the image in your mind. You are not alone.

CHAPTER 7
A—ADJUST: PART 1 -
NAVIGATING CHANGE
WITH CONFIDENCE

If we don't change, we don't grow. If we don't grow, we aren't really living."

– Anatole France

AT THIS POINT IN THE BOOK, I HOPE YOU HAVE LEARNED MUCH more about how stress impacts you mentally and physically; you have identified your stressors, your stress signals and symptoms, and how to measure your stress level. I hope you have been more aware of yourself—your body, your mind, and your needs. I hope you have identified the strategies that work well for managing your stress. I hope you have identified the areas in your life that need to be adjusted for you to have the life God promised: a life of abundance of peace, happiness, and joy. To experience happiness and joy, we must know our needs and work toward creating the life that works well for us. It does not and cannot happen by chance; we have to create it. God gave us some insight into this concept of completing the necessary steps to experience joy and happiness in John 15:10–13 (NLT), which says, "When you obey my commandments, you remain in my love, just as I obey my Father's commandments and remain in his love. I have told you these things so that you will be filled with my joy. Yes, your joy will overflow!"

John 15 begins with Jesus as the vine and us being connected to Him to live. We always need to do something to get the results we desire.

Keeping God's commandments—about how to live morally; how to treat others; and how to take care of our bodies, His temples; and how to connect with Him daily—results in joy that overflows! That is a promise; God never breaks His promises!

Have you ever thought of creating commandments for your life? Of creating a set of principles that are unique to your needs, and when you complete them, you experience joy and peace? What steps must you follow to reduce your stress and have peace of mind? The self-assessments you completed in the preceding chapters should have helped you to identify what triggers you, the coping strategies that work for you, and how to take care of your health through sleep, nutrition, exercise, and balance. Now that you have the knowledge, the next step is transformation. You will begin the process of creating your Individualized Stress Management Plan.

YOUR PERSONALIZED STRESS MANAGEMENT PLAN (PSMP)

My 10 commandments and principles for managing stress.

See Appendix VIII for a Personalized Stress Management Plan (PSMP) template that you can complete.

Commandments	Response
I will pay attention to my stress levels by noticing my stress symptoms when my body gives me the signal. My symptoms and signals are:	
I will not ignore my stress signals and symptoms! I will respond to them and implement my relaxation strategies, which are:	
After implementing my relaxation strategies, I will assess and identify my stressors. My stressors are:	

Commandments	Response
I will categorize my stressors to create a plan for the things I can control and release the things I cannot control. (a) The things I can control are: (b) The things I cannot control are:	
I will make time to process and resolve any issues that are causing me to feel unsettled or rob my peace. My resolutions are:	
I will prioritize my health by making time to make nutritious meals that make me feel healthy and energized. These meals are:	
I will prioritize exercise weekly for at least thirty minutes to improve my body's functioning and produce serotonin naturally. My ideal exercise routine and the best times to exercise are:	
I will practice good sleep hygiene that will help me to feel rested and have a balanced mood. My bedtime routine will be:	
I will identify the areas of priority in my life (myself, family, work, spirituality, friendships, community, special interests, etc.) and determine how much time and commitment they require to create balance. a. The areas in my life that I will prioritize are: b. My daily and weekly schedule to create balance in my life is as follows:	

Commandments	Response
I will accept God's plan for me to live an abundant and fulfilling life by: Participating in the following self-care activities: Connecting with the following people who love me and who I love: Engaging in the following activities that bring me joy and lots of laughter:	

TRANSFORMATION

After you have created your Personalized Stress Management Plan, the next step is implementing the plan to get your desired outcome. Transformation can refer to any process or change that results in a significant shift or alteration in something, whether it's a physical object, a system, an organization, or even a person's beliefs or behavior.

Change can be scary. Change can cause us to feel fearful because of its unknown element. Then you add in our skillful ability to create the worst possible outcomes in our heads, which increase and multiply our fears. We are fixated on the what-ifs, the maybes, the coulds, and the shoulds. Before we know it, we are running for the hills, and it's all in our heads. Change can also be painful because of the type of change, such as losing a loved one, losing a job, or having difficulty functioning normally because of health challenges. The reality is that we have to adjust to things daily because situations happen that are totally outside of our control. However, knowing strategies to help us navigate changes better will ultimately help us to reduce stress and increase our quality of life.

It is unlikely that you can experience transformation without some form of adjustment. Transformation, by definition, involves a significant change or alteration, and such changes often require adjustment to fully realize the benefits of the transformation.

For example, suppose you are trying to transform your physical health and fitness. In that case, you may need to adjust your diet, exercise routine, and lifestyle habits to achieve your goals. Similarly, suppose you are trying to transform your organization. In that case, you may need to adjust your strategy, structure, culture, and operations to achieve your desired outcomes.

Adjustment can be difficult and may involve some discomfort or resistance, especially if the change is significant or requires you to let go of old habits or ways of thinking. However, it is often necessary to fully realize your transformation's benefits and sustain the change over the long term.

The word *adjust* means to make changes or alterations to something to improve its performance, functionality, or fit. Overall, adjusting involves making changes in response to new information or circumstances to ensure a better fit or outcome.

When we think of adjustment, we must consider the internal and external impact of change. How do you respond to a change in your mind and body, and how do the people around you respond to the changes you are making? Managing ourselves internally impacts how effectively we respond to change. Internally, it is helpful to be aware of whether or not you embrace change, regardless of the discomfort, or if you avoid change because it makes you feel uncomfortable or afraid. Another internal consideration is your mental health stability before embarking on a major change in your life. If you are struggling with a mental illness, such as major depression or a psychotic disorder, it will help to ensure that you are maintaining your treatment and feel stable before making major adjustments in your life. Changes can sometimes be stressful and overwhelming depending on the type of change, so it is important to have stability in your mood and thoughts.

Some changes that you make may impact the people and systems in your life. It is important to be aware of how you respond to people and systems in your life who may not agree with your changes. Do you struggle with setting boundaries? Is saying no, or I can't right now, difficult for you? Do you struggle with guilt or people-pleasing? It will prove very difficult for you to implement your personalized stress management plan and experience the happiness you deserve without having the ability to set healthy boundaries without guilt or choosing to cave in.

INTERNAL CHALLENGES

Adjustment can be difficult because it often requires us to step out of our comfort zones and face new challenges. We struggle with adjusting for various reasons. Take a look at the list below and identify the reasons why adjustment has been difficult for you. (Write on the lines below any options you do not see on this list.)

- ☐ **Feeling unsettling:** Adjusting to a new situation, such as a new job, a new city, or a new relationship, can be unsettling and cause feelings of anxiety or stress.

- ☐ **Loss of familiarity:** Adjusting to a new environment can also mean losing the comfort of familiarity. When individuals are used to a certain routine or set of expectations, changing them can be challenging.

- ☐ **Fear of the unknown:** The fear of the unknown can also make adjustment difficult. Individuals may worry about what will happen in a new situation or how they will cope with new challenges.

- ☐ **Lack of control:** When individuals are faced with a new situation, they may feel like they have less control over their lives, which can be unsettling.

- ☐ **Limited resources:** Adjusting to a new situation may require individuals to learn new skills or develop new habits, which can be difficult if they lack the necessary resources, such as time or support.

- ☐ _____
- ☐ _____
- ☐ _____

What did you identify as possible reasons that change may be challenging and cause you to pull back and avoid it? Is it feeling unsettled? Loss of familiarity due to change in your routine? Fear of the unknown being worse than your present circumstances? Are you afraid of losing control because of having to learn new ways of functioning? Lack of financial, emotional, or physical resources that would impact the implementation of your plan?

The reality is that adjusting and changing creates anxiety for various reasons, which can impact the transformation process for better or worse. I want to reassure you that struggling with change is not unique to you; it is prevalent and can be very debilitating depending on the circumstances or situations and the individual.

Did You Know?

Did you know that adjustment disorder is a diagnosis in the American Psychiatric Association's Diagnostic and Statistical Manual of Mental Disorders, Fifth Edition (DSM-5)?[28]

Adjustment disorders are stress-related conditions. You experience more stress than would normally be expected in response to a stressful or unexpected event, which causes significant problems in your relationships, work, or school.

Work problems, going away to school, an illness, the death of a close family member, or any number of life changes can cause stress. Most of the time, people adjust to such changes within a few months. But if you have an adjustment disorder, you continue to have emotional or behavioral reactions that can contribute to feeling anxious or depressed.[29]

Adjustment disorder is diagnosed when an individual experiences significant distress or impairment in functioning within three months of a stressful life event, such as a job loss, divorce, or health problems.[30]

It's difficult to provide an exact statistic for the number of Americans diagnosed with adjustment disorder, because it can be challenging to diagnose and is often underreported. However, studies suggest that adjustment disorder is a relatively common mental health condition, accounting for up to 20 percent of mental health diagnoses in outpatient settings.

Additionally, adjustment disorder is more common among individuals who have experienced traumatic or stressful events, such as veterans or survivors of natural disasters. Some estimates suggest that up to 50 percent of individuals who experience a traumatic event may develop adjustment disorder.

Adjustment disorder is a common mental health condition that can affect individuals of any age, gender, or background. Suppose you or someone you know is experiencing symptoms of adjustment disorder. In that case, seeking professional help from a mental health provider is important.

SYMPTOMS OF ADJUSTMENT DISORDER

Signs and symptoms depend on the type of adjustment disorder and can vary from person to person. You experience more stress than would normally be expected in response to a stressful event, and the stress causes significant problems in your life.

Adjustment disorders affect how you feel and think about yourself and the world and may also affect your actions or behavior. Some examples include the following.

- Feeling sad, hopeless, or not enjoying things you used to enjoy
- Frequent crying
- Worrying or feeling anxious, nervous, jittery, or stressed out
- Trouble sleeping
- Lack of appetite

- Difficulty concentrating
- Feeling overwhelmed
- Difficulty functioning in daily activities
- Withdrawing from social supports
- Avoiding important things, such as going to work or paying bills
- Suicidal thoughts or behavior

Symptoms of an adjustment disorder start within three months of a stressful event and last no longer than six months after the end of the stressful event. However, persistent or chronic adjustment disorders can continue for more than six months, especially if the stressor is ongoing, such as unemployment.

Managing life stressors in or outside of your control requires adjustment. So, we adjust daily to manage what life places at our feet. On the other hand, deciding to intentionally create change in your life can also become stressful in the initial stages. You need to be aware of your challenges with adjustment and coping strategies that help you to navigate the challenges and when you need professional support if you are not adjusting well to a change.

THE BUTTERFLY: GET READY TO FLY

Change can be compared to a caterpillar's transformation into a butterfly. Just as a caterpillar goes through a challenging process of breaking down its old body and rebuilding it into something entirely new, change often involves breaking down old habits, beliefs, and ways of thinking to create a better version of ourselves.

This transformation may be difficult and uncomfortable, but it is necessary for growth and can lead to something beautiful and awe-inspiring. Just as a butterfly emerges from its cocoon, we can emerge from our struggles and challenges as stronger and more resilient individuals. And just as a butterfly's wings are a thing of beauty, the positive changes we make in our lives can be truly remarkable and inspiring to those around us.

STRATEGIES WHEN FEELING UNSETTLED OR ANXIOUS

Adjusting to a new situation can be challenging and unsettling, but there are several things you can do to cope with the stress and anxiety that may come with change. Following are some strategies that may help.

* **Acknowledge your feelings:** It's normal to feel anxious or stressed when faced with a new situation. Don't try to suppress or ignore these feelings; instead, acknowledge them and accept them as a natural response to change. (Scan code to watch the video "Anxiety Is Your Friend").

* **Pray and read God's promises:** Review God's words of encouragement for fears, tell Him how you feel, and allow him to give you His peace and strength to move forward. Here are the steps to God's peace in Philippians 4:6–9 (NKJV).

> Be anxious for nothing, but in everything by prayer and supplication, with thanksgiving, let your requests be made known to God. The peace of God, which surpasses all understanding, will guard your hearts and minds through Christ Jesus. Finally, brethren, whatever things are true, whatever things are noble, whatever things are just, whatever things are pure, whatever things are lovely, whatever things are of good report, if there is any virtue and if there is anything praiseworthy—meditate on these things. The things you learned and received, heard and saw in me, these do, and the God of peace will be with you.

* **Focus on the positives:** Even though change can be difficult, it can also bring new opportunities and experiences. As the Bible verse suggested above, "Whatever things are pure, whatever things are lovely, whatever things are of good report, if there is any virtue and if there is anything praiseworthy—meditate on these things." Try to focus on the positives of the situation and look for ways to embrace the change and make the most of it.

* **Self-talk:** Utilize self-talk to remind yourself of the positives whenever negative thoughts and feelings about the change enter your mind.

* **Take small steps:** Rather than trying to tackle everything at once, break the change down into smaller, more manageable steps. This can help you feel less overwhelmed and more in control.

* **Stay connected:** It's important to maintain social connections during a change period. Reach out to friends, family, or colleagues for support and to stay connected to your community.

* **Practice self-care:** Taking care of yourself during periods of change is essential. Make sure that you're getting enough rest, exercise, and healthy food. Consider practicing your relaxation techniques, such as meditation or deep breathing, to help manage stress.

* **Seek professional support:** If you're struggling to cope with the stress and anxiety of a new situation, consider seeking professional support from a therapist or counselor. They can provide you with additional coping strategies and support as you navigate the change.

LOSS OF FAMILIARITY/STEPPING OUT OF YOUR COMFORT ZONE

Coping with the loss of familiarity during change can be difficult, but several strategies can help you to adjust to your new environment.

* **Be patient with yourself:** Remember that adjusting to a new environment takes time. Be patient with yourself and don't expect to feel completely comfortable or at home right away.

* **Embrace the new environment:** Instead of focusing on what you've lost, embrace the new environment and explore what it offers. Look for new experiences, activities, and opportunities that you might not have had in your old environment.

* **Create new routines:** Establishing new routines can help you to feel more grounded and in control of your new environment. Start by identifying the most important things to you and finding ways to incorporate them into your new routine.

* **Stay connected to familiar people and places:** While you may be in a new environment, it doesn't mean you have to leave everything from your old environment behind. Stay in touch with familiar people and places, whether it's through phone calls, video chats, or visits.

* **Seek out support:** Adjusting to a new environment can be challenging, but you don't have to do it alone. Reach out to friends, family, or colleagues for support and to stay connected to your community.

* **Keep an open mind:** Change can be uncomfortable but brings new opportunities and experiences. Keep an open mind, be willing to try new things, and meet new people in your new environment.

By practicing these strategies, you can help make the transition to your new environment smoother and less overwhelming.

FEAR OF THE UNKNOWN (WHAT-IFS / MAYBES)

Coping with the fear of the unknown can be challenging, but several strategies can help you manage your anxiety and make the decision to make a change.

* **Identify your fears:** Start by identifying your specific fears or concerns about the change. Write them down and try to understand where they are coming from.

* **Gather information:** Once you've identified your fears, gather as much information as you can about the situation. Research the new environment, talk to people who have gone through similar changes, and ask questions to alleviate any concerns you may have.

* **Make a plan:** Having a plan can help you to feel more in control and confident about the change. Identify the steps you need to take to prepare for the change and create a timeline or schedule to help you stay on track.

* **Practice visualization:** Visualization can be a powerful tool for managing anxiety and building confidence. Imagine yourself overcoming any challenges that may arise. Try visualizing yourself in the new situation, feeling confident and successful.

* **Seek support:** Talking to friends, family, or a therapist can help to manage anxiety and gain perspective on the change. Consider contacting a support group or online community of people who have undergone similar changes.

* **Focus on the present moment:** Instead of getting caught up in worries about the future, or the past, focus on the present moment. Remember we cannot change the past or control the future; however, we can be intentional about the here and now.

By practicing these strategies, you can help manage your anxiety and build confidence as you make the decision to make a change. Remember that change can be challenging but can also bring new opportunities and experiences that can enrich your life.

LACK OF CONTROL

Feeling a lack of control when making a change can be difficult, but several strategies can help you manage these feelings.

* **Identify what you can control:** Start by identifying the things that you can control in the new situation. Make a list of the tasks or decisions that are within your power and focus on these things as you navigate the change.

* **Let go of what you can't control:** Recognize that there will be aspects of the new situation that are beyond your control. Let go of these things and focus your energy on the things you can control.

* **Stay organized:** Creating a plan or schedule can help you to feel more in control and organized. Break down tasks into smaller, manageable steps, and focus on one thing at a time.

* **Practice self-care:** It is essential to take care of yourself during periods of change. Make sure you're getting enough rest, exercise, and healthy food. Consider practicing relaxation techniques, such as meditation or deep breathing, to help manage stress.

* **Seek support:** Don't be afraid to ask for help or support from friends, family, or colleagues. Sometimes, having someone to talk to can make all the difference in helping you feel more in control.

* **Focus on your values:** Remember your values and what is important to you in life. Focusing on your values can help you to stay grounded and centered during times of change and can guide you in making decisions that are true to who you are.

By practicing these strategies, you can help to manage feelings of a lack of control and feel more empowered as you navigate the change. Remember that change can be challenging but can also bring new opportunities and experiences that can enrich your life.

LIMITED RESOURCES

When facing limited resources when making a change, it's important to approach the situation with a positive and proactive mindset. Following are some strategies that can help you cope with limited resources when adjusting to a new situation:

* **Prioritize:** Identify the most important skills or habits you need to learn or develop to succeed in the new situation. Prioritizing will help you focus your energy and resources on the most important things.

* **Be resourceful:** Identify the resources you have and the resources you need. Seek support from your network of family and friends, government programs, organizations, and so on. Look for creative ways to access the resources you need.

* **Set realistic goals:** When learning new skills or developing new habits, it's important to set achievable goals, given your available resources. Break larger goals into smaller, more manageable steps, and focus on making daily progress. Adjust your timeline based on your resources.

* **Be patient and persistent:** Change takes time and effort, and it's important to be patient and persistent as you work toward your goals. Celebrate small victories along the way, and don't be discouraged by setbacks or obstacles.

* **Take care of yourself:** Making a change can be stressful, so taking care of yourself is important. Ensure you get enough sleep, eat healthy, and take breaks when needed.

By practicing these strategies, you can help overcome concerns about limited resources and develop the skills and habits you need to adjust to the new situation. Remember that change can be challenging, but you can succeed with the right mindset and approach.

FINAL TIPS FOR MANAGING CHANGES INTERNALLY

1. **Embrace:** Embrace the nervous/anxious feelings; they are normal. The feelings are your body's way of telling you that you are about to embark on new territory.

2. **Relax:** Use your personalized relaxation strategy to calm yourself down; you need a clear mind.

3. **Respond:** Respond to the signal that your body is giving you by asking yourself why you are making this decision. Write down the pros and cons.

4. **Decide:** If you are reassured about your decision, make the move. If you are not reassured and see evidence that it might not be the right choice or timing, go back to the drawing board and improve on your plan.

Don't Run: When it gets difficult, utilize all the coping strategies you have learned and push through. Try not to avoid it.

Did You Know?

The time it takes to develop a new habit can vary depending on several factors, including the complexity of the habit, the individual's personality and motivation, and the consistency of the habit practice. Research suggests that, on average, it takes about sixty-six days for a new habit to become automatic, although the range can be anywhere from eighteen to 254 days, depending on the individual and the habit in question.

It's important to note that developing a habit is not just about repetition but also about creating cues and rewards that reinforce the behavior. For example, if you're trying to establish a habit of exercising every morning, you might create a cue by setting out your workout clothes the night before and a reward by treating yourself to a healthy breakfast afterward.

In general, the key to developing a new habit is consistency and persistence. By practicing the behavior consistently, even in small ways, over time, you can rewire your brain to make the behavior more automatic and natural. It's also important to be patient with yourself and not get discouraged if it takes longer than expected to develop the habit. With time and effort, you can develop the habits that will help you to achieve your goals and improve your life.

REMEMBER

Your transformation may be difficult and uncomfortable, but it is necessary for growth and can lead to something beautiful and awe-inspiring. Just as a butterfly emerges from its cocoon, you can emerge from your struggles and challenges as a stronger and more resilient individual. And just as a butterfly's wings are a thing of beauty, the positive changes you make in your life can be truly remarkable and inspiring to those around you.

FLY

I hope this chapter has helped you be more prepared to make the changes you need in your life. One of the most important points I wanted to convey was that change can be difficult. When we appreciate the challenges that creating changes can present, we will invest in being prepared to navigate the changes by increasing self-awareness and utilizing strategies that work for us. I hope you feel empowered to implement your Personalized Stress Management Plan, which is the 10 commandments for your life. It's your time to FLY.

CHAPTER 8

A—ADJUST:
PART 2- EMBRACING YOUR WORTH AND SETTING HEALTHY BOUNDARIES

IN THIS CHAPTER, I WANT TO ADDRESS THE EXTERNAL AND some internal considerations for boundaries. It is difficult to set boundaries externally if we do not respect our internal boundaries, which are our needs. We have to feel comfortable and peaceful honoring ourselves before we can request that others honor our desires. A lot of self-dishonoring stems from childhood. Some people were made to believe as children that their feelings do not matter, that they are not capable of making their own decisions, or that being selfless is ignoring and trampling on your feelings and elevating the feelings and needs of others. Setting healthy boundaries is contrary to those feelings. Therefore, to develop the skill and ability to set healthy boundaries, we must first develop self-love and self-worth.

SELF-LOVE

Many people believe and have been taught that self-love is un-Christ-like. The truth is Christ has nothing to do with that belief. Let's look at some scriptural references to self-love in the Bible.

"Love your neighbor as yourself." This commandment, found in Mark 12:31 (NLT), implies that we should love ourselves first before we can love others.

"You shall love your neighbor as yourself." This is a similar commandment to the first one and is found in Matthew 22:39 (NKJV).

"You shall love the Lord your God with all your heart, and with all your soul, and with all your mind. This is the great first commandment. And a second is like it: 'You shall love your neighbor as yourself.'" This passage from Matthew 22:37–39 (NKJV) emphasizes the importance of self-love as a prerequisite to loving others.

"And do not be conformed to this world, but be transformed by the renewing of your mind, that by testing you may prove what is that good and acceptable and perfect will of God." This verse from Romans 12:2 (NKJV) suggests that we need to renew our minds and attitudes toward ourselves to discern God's will for our lives.

"For you formed my inward parts; You covered me in my mother's womb. I will praise You, for I am fearfully and wonderfully made. Marvelous are Your works, And that my soul knows very well." This passage from Psalm 139:13–14 (NKJV) reminds us that we are fearfully and wonderfully made by God and that we should appreciate ourselves as His creation.

"Or do you not know that your body is a temple of the Holy Spirit who is in you, whom you have from God, and you are not your own? For you were bought at a price; therefore, glorify God in your body and in your spirit, which are God's." This verse from 1 Corinthians 6:19–20 (NKJV) highlights the importance of valuing our bodies as a temple of the Holy Spirit and caring for ourselves physically and spiritually.

The Scriptures indicate that it is impossible to truly love others without loving ourselves. Loving ourselves should not be confused with the idea of outward beauty only and based only on comparisons to others to validate our worth. Loving ourselves should stem from the value God places on you. He created us with intricate care, details, and beauty. God took His time with us; He was intentional with every single detail. We were created with such complexity that we continue to confuse and confound the best scientists because our composition is still not fully understood. Our love for ourselves and our worth should not be based on human standards or validation but on God's worth. The apostle Paul asked the question in 1 Corinthians 6:19 (NKJV): "Or do you not know that your body is a temple of the Holy Spirit within you, whom you have from God, and you are not your own?" This text emphasizes that you are God's, and He dwells within you. That's amazing, isn't it? Then Paul reminds us in verse 20 why we should hold ourselves in high esteem and value: "For you were bought at a price; therefore, glorify God in your body and in your spirit, which are God's." What was the price? The crucifixion of our Lord and Savior Jesus Christ. Therefore, taking care of our mental health glorifies God, and taking care of our physical health glorifies God; our bodies are His temple. Managing our stressors and living a balanced healthy life is not a fad; it is a God-given expectation; our bodies are His temple.

With all the demands of life, it is almost impossible to honor God with our bodies without saying no to things that cause us harm eventually; thus the necessity of healthy boundaries.

BOUNDARIES

In the context of life, boundaries are personal limits and guidelines that we set for ourselves and communicate to others. These limits define what is acceptable and unacceptable behavior, actions, and attitudes toward us and help us to establish healthy relationships with ourselves and others.

Boundaries can come in various forms, such as physical, emotional, and mental boundaries. Physical boundaries involve setting limits on how close others can come to us or touch us. Emotional boundaries relate to our feelings, values, and beliefs and involve setting limits on how we allow others to treat us emotionally. Mental boundaries involve setting limits on how much information and input we allow others to have in our lives and decisions.

Setting and maintaining boundaries is essential to self-care and self-respect, as it helps us avoid being taken advantage of, manipulated, or mistreated by others. By setting and communicating our boundaries clearly and assertively, we can create a safe and healthy environment for ourselves and cultivate meaningful relationships with others based on mutual respect and understanding.

Following are some steps to set healthy boundaries in the context of life.

* **Identify your values and needs:** Take time to reflect on what is important to you and what you need to feel happy and fulfilled. This can help you establish clear boundaries that align with your values and needs.

* **Recognize your limits:** Be aware of your limits and what you can and cannot tolerate in your relationships and interactions with others. This can help you to establish boundaries that protect your well-being.

* **Communicate your boundaries clearly:** Once you have identified your boundaries, communicate them clearly and assertively to others. Be specific about what you are comfortable with and what you are not, and be firm in enforcing your boundaries. Enforcing your boundaries should not be done aggressively or by force. Enforcing your boundaries assertively involves communicating your needs with confidence and choosing to walk away or not interact with someone as a consequence of not respecting your needs. You cannot control the behaviors of others; however, you can control yourself.

* **Practice self-care:** Take care of yourself physically, emotionally, and mentally. This can help you feel more confident and empowered to set and enforce your boundaries.

* **Be consistent:** Once you have established your boundaries, be consistent in enforcing them. This can help you avoid confusion and misunderstandings with others and maintain healthy relationships.

* **Respect other people's boundaries:** Just as you have the right to set boundaries, so do others. Respect their boundaries and communicate with them in a way that is respectful and considerate of their needs and values.

* **Be willing to adjust your boundaries as needed:** Your boundaries may change over time as your needs and circumstances change. Be open to adjusting your boundaries as needed to ensure they continue to align with your values and needs.

OVERCOMING GUILT

Guilt is a complex emotional state that arises from the belief or perception that one has violated a moral or ethical standard or has failed to meet an expectation or obligation. It can be experienced as a sense of remorse, regret, or self-blame, often involving shame, anxiety, or sadness. Guilt can be triggered by various factors, including personal actions or inactions, social norms, cultural values, or religious beliefs.

Setting boundaries can be challenging, especially when it involves saying no to someone or distancing ourselves from others who may not respect our boundaries. This can often lead to feelings of guilt or anxiety about hurting others' feelings.

Guilt is an emotion that is often displaced—especially in the context of boundary-setting. Your guilt may be self-inflicted when you feel guilty because someone responds with distress when you communicate your boundary. Or your guilt may be inflicted on you by other people who may attempt to "guilt trip" you by telling you that your actions are selfish and can cause you to question your decision.

Displaced guilt is a psychological phenomenon that can occur in the context of boundary setting. When a person sets a boundary with someone else, such as saying no to a request or establishing a limit on what they are willing to tolerate, it can sometimes trigger feelings of guilt.

Displaced guilt occurs when a person experiences guilt for setting a boundary, even though the boundary is reasonable and necessary for their well-being. This guilt may be displaced from another source, such as a childhood experience where the person was made to feel guilty for asserting their needs or desires.

For example, a person may feel guilty for setting a boundary with a friend who frequently asks for favors, even though they feel overwhelmed and need to prioritize their own needs. This guilt may stem from an earlier experience where the person was made to feel guilty for not putting others' needs ahead of their own.

Displaced guilt can be a barrier to setting healthy boundaries and can lead to you tolerating unacceptable behavior or feeling responsible for the emotions and actions of others. To overcome displaced guilt, it may be helpful to explore the source of the guilt, practice self-compassion, and remind yourself that it is okay to prioritize your own needs and well-being.

REGRET

A more appropriate emotion to feel when someone is distressed when your boundaries are communicated may be regret. Regret is defined as a feeling of disappointment or sorrow over something that has happened or that one has done or failed to do. It typically involves a sense of loss or missed opportunity and can be directed toward oneself or others. Although regret is also a negative emotion, it might be easier to process because it removes the element of "I am responsible." So, you may regret that someone you care about does not accept your boundary and cuts you out of their life because it is sad; however, you are not responsible for their actions; they are responsible for walking away.

REMEMBER

Taking care of yourself is necessary for your well-being. If someone is hurt by your need, it is unfortunate and regretful; however, your intent is not to hurt them. Guilt is an emotion that you should feel if you intentionally did something to violate or hurt someone else.

Therefore, you should not be feeling guilty; it is okay and healthy to prioritize your needs and well-being. You can attempt to reassure that person that it is not your desire to hurt them if they allow it; however, you would not be seeking forgiveness.

In summary, while both guilt and regret involve negative feelings about past actions or decisions, guilt is more focused on a sense of moral or ethical responsibility to do right by someone else after you have wronged them, while regret is more focused on a sense of loss or missed opportunity.

Following are some ways to cope with guilt when setting boundaries in the context of life

* **Recognize the importance of self-care:** It's important to remember that setting boundaries is not selfish but rather an act of self-care and self-respect. By setting boundaries, you are prioritizing your well-being and mental health.

* **Accept your feelings:** It's okay to feel regret or anxiety when setting boundaries. Acknowledge your feelings without judgment and remind yourself that they are a natural part of the process.

* **Reframe your thoughts:** Instead of viewing boundaries as a harmful or hurtful action, try reframing your thoughts to see them as a positive step toward building healthier relationships and protecting your well-being.

* **Practice self-compassion:** Be kind and compassionate toward yourself, especially when you are feeling guilty or anxious. Treat yourself as you would treat a good friend, with kindness and understanding.

* **Communicate clearly and respectfully:** When setting boundaries, it's important to communicate clearly and respectfully to avoid misunderstandings and hurt feelings. Be honest and direct but also kind and considerate of the other person's feelings.

* **Seek support:** Reach out to a trusted friend or therapist for support when setting boundaries if it becomes challenging for you. Talking to someone who understands and supports your decision can help alleviate feelings of guilt or anxiety.

Remember that setting boundaries is an essential aspect of self-care and self-respect, and it's okay to prioritize your well-being over others' expectations or demands. Setting and enforcing boundaries can become easier and more natural with time and practice, leading to healthier and more fulfilling relationships.

CHAPTER 9

L—LIVE, LOVE, LAUGH
WALKING WITH CHRIST, EMBRACING LOVE, AND CELEBRATING JOY

The thief's purpose is to steal and kill and destroy. My purpose is to give them a rich and satisfying life. (John 10:10 NLT)

IN JOHN 10, JESUS USES ALLEGORY, WHICH IS A STORY, POEM, or picture that can be interpreted to reveal a hidden meaning, to help us understand how to attain a happy, satisfying life. He speaks of a sheep and a shepherd and thieves that come to kill the sheep. The shepherd enters through the gate while the thief sneaks in. The shepherd's intent is to take care of the sheep; the thief's only intent is to deceive and kill the sheep. The shepherd calls His sheep, and they answer and come to Him and follow Him. The sheep run from the thief. Jesus introduces Himself as the Good Shepherd who will protect His sheep from wolves, die for His sheep, and not abandon them; while in contrast, someone who is just hired to care for the sheep will not sacrifice their lives for the sheep because they do not belong to them.

In verses 8 and 9 (NLT), He says, "All who came before me were thieves and robbers. But the true sheep did not listen to them. Yes, I am the gate. Those who come in through me will be saved. They will come and go freely and will find good pastures." Here He confirms and emphasizes that the way to have a happy life is through Him. If we follow Him and His ways, we will find good pasture. Good pasture is green and luscious, symbolizing plenty, fruitfulness, and abundance. The message is consistent with Jesus's advice in John 15: 9–11: "I have loved you even as the Father has loved me. Remain in my love. When you obey my commandments, you remain in my love, just as I obey my Father's commandments and remain in his love. I have told you these things so that you will be filled with my joy. Yes, your joy will overflow!"

I introduced this chapter with biblical references because I truly believe that Jesus is the only way to true joy and happiness. There are many proposed steps and paths that are suggested and recommended for life, love, and joy. However, I choose to follow the path that God has suggested. It is important that, as individuals, we choose our moral pathway on which to hang our values and life choices. When we choose our paths, it is also important that we respect the paths that others have chosen and do not judge them. The information that I share in this chapter on maintaining a life of joy and happiness will be in the context of following Christ's blueprint for happiness.

REALLY LIVING

Our lives cannot be somebody else's; if they are, we are not really living. The R.E.A.L. Stress Management Strategy provides the steps to live a fulfilling life. It's not just a slogan. It details how to go deep and really assess your needs and create a plan to live a life that works for you. At this point in the process, you would have learned about how stress impacts your body, identified your stress signals and symptoms, identified your relaxation techniques, identified your stressors, learned how to categorize your stressors, prioritized the stressors you plan to address, identified coping skills to control your thoughts, created a routine to have good nutrition and exercise, created your ten commandments for your life, and understand the benefits of balance, self-care, and boundaries in your life. You would have hopefully begun the process of planning to implement your plans, armed with skills to manage the challenges of change.

When you begin to implement your plan and have overcome the challenges that come with change, you should start to see the effects of your new plan. You should feel more peaceful, happy, and fulfilled in areas of your life where you were struggling previously. Taking the time to understand yourself and your needs and ensuring that they are aligned with God's plan for you will result in you experiencing the joy and happiness that God has promised.

You begin really living when you are structuring your life to honor your values and priorities; you are respecting your body by responding to the signals it gives you instead of ignoring and pushing through them; you are managing your stressors with God's help and whatever support and professional resources you may need instead of avoiding them; you are setting healthy boundaries with yourself and people around you; and you have created a routine for life that is balanced and acknowledges God as your source. Sometimes we structure our lives based on the belief that our plans will only be executed effectively solely by our own abilities, and we become determined to achieve our success by doing everything in our own power. However, when we understand that we don't have the control God does, and that He actually wants us to be successful and win, then we will not overexert ourselves. We would allow Him to help us. I imagined this image in my head of us running around, tiring ourselves out, and messing things up. Then God taps us on the shoulder and says with a smile, "May I help you?" What will happen if we realize and accept that God is all-powerful and that we have divine power at our fingertips? This is what will happen: We will have a front-row seat to the miracles He will work in our lives, become the beneficiaries of his bountiful blessings, and experience great success. With this approach of relying on the divine, we would have time to spend with God in prayer and praise and to wait for Him to talk back to us instead of rushing to go and figure out life on our own. God shared these words with Zerubbabel in Zechariah 4:6 (NKJV): "So he answered and said to me: 'This is the word of the Lord to Zerubbabel: Not by might nor by power, but by My Spirit,' says the Lord of hosts."

Sometimes we hustle so hard and work so hard at the expense of hurting our bodies and neglecting our families and friends. Before we know it, our relationships are strained and distant. We are struggling with so many health issues we can't even manage. All the while, God is waiting for us to allow Him through the power of the Holy Spirit to fulfill the purpose and plans He has destined for us to achieve and receive.

Let's resist the urge to do life on our own and chase things that give temporal gain, and instead, take God's hand and let Him show us the way.

God gives one of the most comforting invitations in Matthew 11:28–30 (NLT). "Then Jesus said, 'Come to me, all of you who are weary and carry heavy burdens, and I will give you rest. Take my yoke upon you. Let me teach you because I am humble and gentle at heart, and you will find rest for your souls. For my yoke is easy to bear, and the burden I give you is light."

Here, the term *yoke* is used metaphorically to refer to the teachings and way of life that Jesus offers to His followers. A yoke was a wooden frame that was used to harness two animals together to pull a plow or cart, and it represented hard work and a heavy burden.

Harnessing two animals together in a yoke was a common practice in agriculture and transportation in many cultures throughout history. The purpose of yoking animals together was to combine their strength and work capacity so that they could pull heavier loads or work more efficiently than a single animal could on its own.

God is giving you the invitation to be yoked to Him, to submit yourself to him, to be joined to Him so that He can lighten your load. God is committing to work with you to accomplish your goals and responsibilities and help you to be more productive and successful than you would by yourself. He promises that His Yoke is "easy" and "His burden is light." Jesus is communicating to us and reassuring us that following Him will not be a burden that is too heavy to bear but rather a source of help, rest, and peace for our souls.

Do you want the rest and peace God is offering? I know that trusting God is not easy; I, too, struggle daily to rely on Him and seek Him first. I think one of the reasons we struggle is because we cannot physically see Him and touch Him. We would more likely trust a car salesman because we can see him than trust God. Maybe it's because you feel He has failed or disappointed you. This is where faith comes in, trusting God even when it hurts and seems confusing. When we believe in a God we cannot see, a God who is all-powerful and all-knowing; we will see the evidence of His love and existence when He manifests His works in our lives.

Have you been yoked to God? Have you been consulting Him about everything that concerns you? Have you been waiting for His answers or instead trying to resolve things on your own? If you have not been yoked to God, I want you to pray this simple prayer: "Lord, I receive and accept your invitation to be yoked to you; please help me to submit to your will, in Jesus' name, amen!"

When we are yoked to God, we reduce our stress levels significantly because we experience the benefits of the God factor in our lives.

LOVE

Everyone desires to be loved and to give love. We were first introduced to love by the family we were born into as children. Our concept of love is largely impacted by how love is expressed to us by our caregivers. As a result, everyone has unique ways in which they give and receive love. What does the topic of love have to do with stress management? The topic of love is relevant to managing stress because of the powerful impact that social connections and positive relationships can have on our stress levels and overall well-being. Studies have shown that there is a strong correlation between love and managing stress. Love and social connections have been found to be essential factors in reducing stress levels and improving overall health and well-being.

Did You Know?

When we experience love and connection with others, our brain releases hormones like oxytocin and dopamine, which can help to reduce stress and promote feelings of relaxation and well-being.

This is why spending time with loved ones, engaging in activities that bring us joy, and nurturing positive relationships are all important ways to manage stress.

On the other hand, when we feel isolated, disconnected from others, rejected, and disappointed in relationships, our stress levels can increase, and we may be more vulnerable to the harmful effects of stress on our health and well-being. It is, therefore, very important to prioritize social connections and relationships with people we love and who make us feel loved.

Sometimes people don't get to experience the benefits of love and social connections. Many factors impact a person's ability or capacity to give and receive love, including the following.

* **Low self-esteem of self-worth:** Some individuals do not believe that they are deserving of love or lovable. As a result, they will avoid deep connections or sabotage opportunities to experience genuine love.

* **Mental health issues:** Individuals who experience mental health issues, such as depression, anxiety, or personality disorders, may have difficulty forming and maintaining relationships. For example, individuals who have experienced trauma or abuse may struggle with forming healthy attachments and building trust in relationships.

✳ **Social isolation:** Some individuals may lack access to social networks or may struggle to form meaningful connections with others due to factors such as living in a rural area, having a disability, or experiencing discrimination or prejudice.

✳ **Life circumstances:** Some individuals may struggle to find time for relationships or social connections due to demanding work schedules, caregiving responsibilities, or other life circumstances that make it challenging to prioritize social interactions.

✳ **Difficulty trusting others:** Some individuals may struggle with connecting with others because of the fear of being hurt or rejected based on past negative experiences.

Review the following checklist to identify potential reasons you may not be experiencing the full benefits of love and connection. There are extra lines to add reasons that may not be on the list.

☐ Low Self-esteem or Self-worth

☐ Mental Health Issues

☐ Social Isolation

☐ Life Circumstances

☐ Difficulty Trusting Others

☐ _____

☐ _____

☐ _____

Identifying and addressing the reasons you may not be experiencing the benefits of love and connection can help reduce stress levels and improve overall health. You can work through these challenges on your own or with the support of a trained mental health professional.

The reality is that love is a vital part of our existence and survival. We were created by a God who loves us and has been fighting for the past 6,000 years to redeem us through His love. You deserve to be loved and experience love because you are loved and were created in love.

The Oxford Dictionary defines love as a feeling of deep affection. A great interest and pleasure in something or a deep affection for (someone).[31]

In researching love, it became clear that most people believed love to be based solely on emotions. The information I gathered revealed that love is often described as a powerful force that can bring people together, overcome differences, and inspire great acts of kindness and generosity.

I would like to explore the Bible's definition of love, which appears to be very different from what I discovered in my research. How does God define love? 1 John 4:7–12 (NKJV) explains in great detail who and what love is.

> Beloved, let us love one another, for love is from God, and everyone who loves is born of God and knows God. He who does not love does not know God, for God is love. In this, the love of God was made manifested toward us, that God sent his only begotten Son into the world, that we might live through Him. In this is love, not that we have loved God, but that he loved us and sent His Son to be the propitiation for our sins. Beloved, if God so loved us, we also ought to love one another. No one has seen God at any time. If we love one another, God abides in us, and His love has been perfected in us.

Let's unpack this: "Love is from God; and everyone who loves is born of God and knows God." So, it seems like we cannot truly understand love or love others if we are not connected to God, who is love.

Our connection with God can sometimes be very limited and sporadic. Our days are filled with so many responsibilities and demands that we sometimes don't even get to talk with God for at least five minutes.

This biblical explanation of love does move us to reflect on how we have been living. Have we been neglecting to connect with the source of love in our pursuit of love? Could that be the reason why we experience challenges with love in our lives? It is truly worth considering what would change in our lives if we spent quality time connecting with God daily to receive His love and learn how to love. David shares the benefits of loving God in Psalm 91:14–16 (NLT): "The Lord says, 'I will rescue those who love me. I will protect those who trust in my name. When they call on me, I will answer; I will be with them in trouble. I will rescue and honor them. I will reward them with a long life and give them my salvation.'"

When we connect to God and give him our full adoration, He promises to rescue us from our emotional pain and love-scarred hearts; to protect us from danger, whatever shape or person it may come in; stay with us when we experience challenges and not abandon us; bless us with reduced stress and good health, which equals long life; and ultimately give us eternal life. These are amazing promises! This is true love! God is promising to give us love that we have never experienced in our lives. (See Appendix IX for more biblical references to God's love for you.)

1 Corinthians chapter 13 explains the biblical steps of how we should love others. This chapter in the Bible is often referred to as the "love chapter," because it provides a detailed description of what love is and what it looks like in practice. Here are some key points from 1 Corinthians 13 about love:

Love is patient and kind (verse 4).

Love does not envy, boast, or become arrogant (verse 4).

Love is not rude or self-seeking (verse 5).

Love is not easily angered and keeps no record of wrongs (verse 5).

Love rejoices in the truth and protects, trusts, hopes, and perseveres (verses 6–7).

Love never fails (verse 8).

The chapter goes on to explain that love is greater than any other spiritual gift or talent, and that without love, even the most impressive accomplishments are meaningless.

Overall, 1 Corinthians 13 provides a powerful and inspiring message about the importance of love in our lives, and it serves as a reminder that love is not merely an emotion but intentional, selfless action.

Below is a list of the twelve qualities of love identified in 1 Corinthians chapter 13 (NLT/NIV). Review the list and identify areas of strengths and areas for growth in your love for others.

- ☐ Love is patient and kind.
- ☐ Love is not jealous or boastful.
- ☐ Love is not proud.
- ☐ Love is not rude.
- ☐ Love is not self-seeking.
- ☐ It is not easily angered; it keeps no record of wrong.
- ☐ Love thinks no evil.
- ☐ Love does not delight in evil but rejoices in the truth.
- ☐ Love never gives up.
- ☐ Love never loses faith.
- ☐ Love is always hopeful.
- ☐ Love endures through every circumstance.

Holding up our character against this list may seem daunting and overwhelming. However, look at verse 9 in 1 John 4 (ESV): "In this the love of God was made manifest among us, that God sent his only Son into the world, so that we might live through him." We cannot love each other without Jesus' help; it is impossible, and we will fall short. We must love through Jesus. Thank God it's not up to us, because we so often get into our heads and feelings!

Pray this prayer with me: Lord, help me to love you and seek after you so that I can experience true love and learn how to love people. Help me to overcome my challenges of giving love and allowing people to love me. Help me to show others the love you show me. In Jesus' name. Amen.

LAUGH

"A merry heart does good, like medicine, but a broken spirit dries the bones" (Proverbs 17:22 NKJV).

This is one of my favorite Bible verses written by King Solomon in the book of Proverbs. It suggests that a positive and joyful outlook can benefit a person's physical and emotional health.

The phrase "a merry heart" refers to a happy and cheerful attitude, and "medicine" represents a cure or remedy for illness. Therefore, the Proverb suggests that having a positive and joyful attitude can have a healing effect on the body and mind.

On the other hand, "a broken spirit" refers to a sense of hopelessness or despair, which can lead to physical and emotional exhaustion. The phrase "dries the bones" implies that a broken spirit can drain a person's vitality and energy, leaving them feeling weak and depleted.

Laughter can be seen as a manifestation of a merry heart, which according to the Proverb, has a positive effect on a person's well-being. Just as medicine can heal the body, a joyful and positive attitude, including laughter, can heal the body and mind.

When we laugh, our bodies release endorphins. These natural, feel-good chemicals can help to reduce stress, relieve pain, and improve our overall mood. Laughter also helps to stimulate the immune system and reduce the levels of stress hormones in the body, which can contribute to improved physical health.

Imagine going to the doctor with a health complaint, and he writes a prescription that reads, "Laughter and a lot of it!" What would you do? You would probably think it was a mistake, or he was not mentally stable or wasting your time.

People generally may not have thought much about how laughter impacts their mental health because it appears to be so simple and "just what we do." However, you would be surprised to learn how a simple laugh that you elicit when you feel happy or cheerful can change the course of your health and reduce your stress levels.

One notable study on the benefits of laughter for managing stress was conducted by Lee Berk and Stanley Tan at Loma Linda University in California. The study, published in the *American Journal of the Medical Sciences* in 2009, examined the effects of laughter on the immune system and stress levels in a group of healthy adults.[32]

In the study, the participants were divided into two groups. One group watched a humorous video while the other watched a non-humorous one. Blood samples were taken from all participants before and after the video viewing to measure levels of stress hormones and immune system markers.

The researchers found that the group who watched the humorous video had lower levels of stress hormones and higher levels of immune system markers compared to the group who watched the non-humorous video.

Specifically, the participants who watched the humorous video had lower cortisol levels. This stress hormone can negatively affect the immune system and higher levels of interleukin-2, which is an immune system protein that helps to fight infection and cancer.[33]

The study's findings suggest that laughter can positively affect both the immune system and stress levels, which can contribute to improved physical and emotional well-being. The study's authors also noted that the positive effects of laughter may be especially beneficial for individuals who experience chronic stress, as chronic stress can have long-term negative effects on the immune system and overall health.

Overall, this study provides evidence for the benefits of laughter in managing stress and promoting overall health, highlighting the potential importance of incorporating humor and laughter into daily life.

Did You Know?

Laughter is a complex physiological response that involves multiple parts of the body. When we perceive something as funny, it triggers a cascade of physical and emotional changes that lead to laughter.

First, the brain processes the information and activates the body's stress response, including releasing hormones such as cortisol and adrenaline. This triggers an increase in heart rate, blood pressure, and breathing rate.

Next, the brain releases endorphins, natural feel-good chemicals that can help to reduce pain, promote relaxation, and improve mood. This leads to a sense of pleasure and enjoyment.

Finally, the muscles in the chest and abdomen contract, leading to a series of rapid, rhythmic movements that produce the characteristic sound of laughter. A laugh is apparently more complex than we think.

Following are some ways in which laughter can help reduce your stress:

* **Laughter reduces stress hormones:** Laughter triggers the release of endorphins, which are the body's natural feel-good chemicals. These endorphins help to reduce stress hormones like cortisol and adrenaline, which can cause physical and emotional stress.

* **Laughter improves immune function:** Studies have shown that laughter can help to boost the immune system by increasing the production of antibodies and activating immune cells like T-cells and natural killer cells. This can help to protect the body from illness and disease.

* **Laughter promotes relaxation**: Laughing can help to relax the body's muscles and reduce tension. This can help to promote feelings of calmness and relaxation, which can counteract the effects of stress.

* **Laughter improves mood:** Laughter has been shown to improve mood and reduce symptoms of depression and anxiety. This is because it increases the production of neurotransmitters like serotonin and dopamine, which are associated with feelings of happiness and well-being.

* **Laughter promotes social bonding:** Laughing with others can help to promote social bonding and strengthen relationships. This can provide a sense of support and connection that can help to reduce feelings of stress and anxiety.

"I haven't laughed like this in a long time!" You may have heard this phrase or repeated it yourself. We usually use this expression when we experience a good belly laugh. Have you had opportunities to laugh lately? Now that you are more aware of how beneficial laughter can be for your overall health and reducing your stress, the next step is to create opportunities to laugh a lot in your life.

CREATING OPPORTUNITIES TO LAUGH A LOT

To experience frequent moments in our lives that cause us to laugh, we have to be intentional about with whom we spend our time, what we spend our time doing, and where we spend our time. Our lives can be super busy, so we have to carve out and schedule time to do things that increase humor in our lives. Now we know that opportunities for laughter should not be an afterthought because it is instrumental to managing our stress and overall well-being. Be aware of the things, activities, people, and places that make you laugh. We are all different, and different things appeal to our senses. Knowing this information will help you to be intentional about scheduling time to create humor in your life.

Following are some ideas on how to create opportunities for laughter in your life:

* **Watch funny movies or TV shows:** Find comedies or humorous shows that you enjoy, and watch them regularly to add some laughter to your day.

* **Read funny books or comics:** Reading humorous books or comics can provide a fun and relaxing escape from everyday stress.

* **Spend time with funny friends or family members:** Spending time with people who have a good sense of humor can be contagious and can lead to many laughs and good times.

* **Attend comedy shows or open mic nights:** Going to live comedy shows or open mic nights can be a fun way to enjoy some laughs and support local comedians.

* **Incorporate humor into daily life:** Look for opportunities to add humor to everyday situations, such as telling jokes, making light of a stressful situation, or finding humor in a mistake.

Remember, laughter is a natural and powerful stress reliever that can provide many benefits for both physical and emotional health. By making an effort to incorporate more humor into your life, you can create opportunities to laugh and enjoy the many benefits of laughter.

My prescription for you is "laughter and a lot of it!"

CHAPTER 10

MAINTAINING HEALTH, WELL-BEING, AND THE BENEFITS OF FLEXIBILITY

I STARTED IN CHAPTER ONE BY SHARING MY JOURNEY AND PUR-suit of happiness after struggling with SAD (Seasonal Affective Disorder). I promised to share with you all the things that God led me to do to manage my stress and reduce and possibly eliminate my symptoms of SAD.

Everything that I shared with you in this book is what I did and am still doing to manage my stress. I hope you have felt empowered to pay more attention to your stress levels and have learned some valuable tools to manage your stress while being yoked to God to experience the God factor.

The process of overcoming depression (SAD) was not a quick one for me; it took time, a lot of praying, a lot of learning about myself, and a lot of courage to move toward making changes to improve my life.

I had no idea that living with a stressor for so long could deteriorate my health in such a drastic way. My overall process to feel joy in my heart and become fully functional again took about two years. I am sharing this with you because it is very important that you are patient with yourself. I remember laughing; however, I did not feel happy. It was surface. I wondered for a while if I would ever feel joy again. Now I laugh, and I feel it! Don't give up on chasing your purpose and the things that bring you joy. The journey will not be without hills and valleys, but you will overcome them because God is with you.

MAINTAINING YOUR HEALTH AND WELLBEING

"The godly may trip seven times, but they will get up again. But one disaster is enough to overthrow the wicked" (Proverbs 24:16 NLT).

When you have created and begun implementing your Personalized Stress Management Plan (PSMP), you will hopefully start to see the results in your overall health and well-being. However, sometimes situations can cause you to not be as committed and diligent in doing things that you know are best for your health. For example, you may experience unexpected stressors in life, such as the loss of a job or loved one, undue stress in many areas of your life, or an illness.Don't be too hard on yourself for not being fully committed to your PSMP. It's completely normal to feel discouraged at times, and I always tell myself and my clients that it's okay to take a moment to process those feelings. Give yourself a few minutes— whether it's literally ten or just enough time to let it out—and acknowledge those emotions. But once that time is up, it's important to remind yourself that perfection isn't the goal, and even a godly person doesn't always have it all together. Set your timer, and when those minutes pass, focus on moving forward with grace and understanding for yourself. Shift mentally to accepting your present state and realize that you will not stay in this space; give yourself grace. Sometimes we hold ourselves back because we do not give ourselves grace. This lack of patience with ourselves sometimes prevents us from receiving God's grace and His support to help us get back on track.

Remember, because you took the time to create your Personalized Stress Management Plan (PSMP), this plan will help you to pinpoint the areas in your life that need improvement and your areas of strength. Once you identify the areas that need improvement, pray for God's help with starting to do them effectively again.

BE FLEXIBLE

Flexibility is especially valuable when navigating life changes, as it helps you adapt to new circumstances and overcome challenges. Being flexible allows you to manage the stress and anxiety that often accompany change by adjusting your expectations and responses to new situations.

The Personalized Stress Management Plan (PSMP) you create today may not be as effective five or ten years later. As humans, we change over time; our likes and dislikes will be different over our lifetime, and that is normal and okay. Life is filled with twists and turns, and we are exposed to different experiences that change how we perceive people and the world around us. This is normal because we should be growing and maturing during our lifetime. For example, imagine you previously enjoyed sugary foods in moderation and were healthy. However, if you develop diabetes, you would need to significantly reduce or eliminate sugary foods from your diet. You would adjust your (PSMP) to minimize sugary food to maintain your health. I know it's easier said than done; however, being flexible with adjusting your nutrition plan would have massive benefits to your health and quality of life.

Be open to adjusting your life based on your current needs. You can count on your body letting you know when things are not okay in your mind and body. The important thing is to pay attention to the signals your body shows you and be willing to adjust.

REVIEW, REFLECT, REASSESS, RECREATE

Review your Individualized Stress Management Plan (PSMP) periodically or if your stress symptoms are high. **Reflect** on what you have been doing to identify what is working and what is no longer effective. **Reassess** your plan and identify possible new ways of coping and any adjustments you may need to make. **Recreate** your plan to suit your present needs and situation.

ALL THE BEST . . .

I pray that these strategies will change your life and help you to begin or continue the journey of living a happy, healthy, fulfilling life. If your life has changed, share this information with the people you love. Remember, trust God to be the leader in your life; do not even attempt to do life without Him. Remember His words of comfort, encouragement, and commitment below in Mathew 6:25–33 (NKJV).

Your Name Here _____

Therefore, I say to you, do not worry about your life, what you will eat or what you will drink, nor about your body, what you will put on. Is not life more than food and the body more than clothing? Look at the birds of the air, for they neither sow nor reap nor gather into barns, and yet your heavenly Father feeds them. Are you not of more value than they? Which of you by worrying, can add one cubit to his stature? So why do you worry about clothing? Consider the lilies of the field, how they grow: they neither toil nor spin, and yet I tell you that even Solomon in all his glory was not arrayed like one of these. Now if God so clothes the grass of the field, which today is, and tomorrow is thrown into the oven, will he not much more clothe you, O you of little faith? Therefore, do not worry, saying, 'What shall we eat?' or 'What shall we drink?' or 'What shall we wear?' For after all these things, the Gentiles seek. For your heavenly Father knows that you need all these things. But seek first the kingdom of God and His righteousness, and all these things will be added to you.

APPENDIX I
(CHAPTER 1)

INFORMATION ON SAD

Seasonal Affective Disorder (SAD) is a type of depression that typically occurs in the fall and winter months when there is less sunlight. SAD is also known as seasonal depression or winter blues.

The symptoms of SAD can vary in severity and may include:

- Low mood, sadness, and hopelessness
- Fatigue, decreased energy, and increased sleepiness
- Increased appetite, especially for carbohydrates
- Weight gain
- Difficulty concentrating and making decisions
- Irritability and moodiness
- Loss of interest in activities that you once enjoyed
- Social withdrawal

These symptoms typically begin in the fall and winter months and improve during the spring and summer months. SAD can also occur in summer, although this is less common.

The exact cause of SAD is not fully understood, but it is thought to be related to reduced exposure to sunlight, which can disrupt the body's internal clock and lead to changes in mood, sleep, and other symptoms.

APPENDIX II
(CHAPTER 4)

TEN TIPS ON FINDING THE RIGHT THERAPIST

Finding the right mental health therapist is an important step in your mental well-being journey. Here are some tips to help you find the right therapist for your needs.

1. **Identify your specific needs:** Determine the type of therapy or issues you want to address. It could be anxiety, depression, trauma, relationship problems, or any other mental health concern. Understanding your needs will help you to find a therapist with expertise in those areas.

2. **Seek referrals and recommendations:** Ask your primary care physician for recommendations. You can also ask trusted friends, family members, or colleagues who have had positive experiences with therapy. Online communities or support groups related to mental health can also provide valuable recommendations.

3. **Research therapists:** Once you have a list of potential therapists, research their credentials, qualifications, and specialties. Check their professional websites and LinkedIn profiles to better understand their work experience history. Read online reviews or testimonials and explore their experience in treating conditions similar to yours.

4. **Consider therapy approaches:** Different therapists use different therapeutic approaches or modalities. Consider what approach aligns with your preferences and needs. Research and understand different therapy approaches like cognitive-behavioral therapy (CBT), psychodynamic therapy, mindfulness-based therapy, etc.

5. **Evaluate their expertise and experience:** Look for therapists who have experience working with clients who have similar concerns to yours. A therapist specializing in your issue is more likely to provide effective treatment.

6. **Verify credentials and licenses:** Ensure the therapist you are considering is licensed and certified and has completed the necessary education and training. Check their credentials with relevant professional licensing boards or organizations.

7. **Consider practical factors:** Think about practical considerations such as location, availability, office hours, and affordability. Choose a therapist who is conveniently located and has availability that fits your schedule. If you have insurance, check if the therapist accepts your insurance or offers sliding scale fees.

8. **Trust your instincts:** After narrowing down your options, schedule initial consultations with a few therapists. Trust your gut feeling during these meetings. Consider how comfortable you feel talking to them and whether you sense a good connection. A good therapeutic relationship is crucial for successful therapy.

9. **Inquire about their approach to therapy:** During the initial consultation, ask the therapist about their approach, treatment plans, and what you can expect from the therapy process. Make sure their approach aligns with your expectations and goals.

10. **Understand the cost and insurance coverage:** Ask about the therapist's fees and if they offer any sliding scale options or payment plans. If you have insurance, contact your insurance provider to understand your mental health coverage and any out-of-pocket costs.

Prioritize your mental health and find a therapist who can support you on your journey to well-being. Remember, finding the right therapist may require some trial and error. It's okay to switch therapists if you feel the current one isn't meeting your needs or if you don't feel comfortable.

APPENDIX III
(CHAPTER 4)

IDENTIFY YOUR STRESSORS

Please use the following form to document your stressors that relate to you. Use the "Other" category to document any stressors not listed below.

WRITE OUT ALL YOUR STRESSORS:

Work-related stressors:

_____

_____

_____

Financial stressors:

_____

_____

_____

Relationship stressors:

_____

_____

_____

Health-related stressors:

_____

_____

_____

Family Stressors:

_____

_____

_____

School stressors:

_____

_____

_____

Personal stressors: negative self-talk, perfectionism, low self-esteem, etc.

_____

_____

_____

Other

_____

_____

_____

APPENDIX IV
(CHAPTER 5)

"YOU ARE MINE"

But now, O _____, listen to the LORD who created you.

O _____, the one who formed you, says,

"Do not be afraid, for I have ransomed you.

I have called you by name; you are mine.

When you go through deep waters,

I will be with you.

When you go through rivers of difficulty,

you will not drown.

When you walk through the fire of oppression,

you will not be burned up;

the flames will not consume you.

For I am the LORD, your God,

the Holy One of Israel, your Savior.

I gave Egypt as a ransom for your freedom;

I gave Ethiopia and Seba in your place.

Others were given in exchange for you.

I traded their lives for yours

because you are precious to me.

You are honored, and I love you.

(Isaiah 43:1–4 NLT)

APPENDIX V
(CHAPTER 5)

CATEGORIZE YOUR STRESSORS

Things You Can Control	Things You Cannot Control

APPENDIX VI

(CHAPTER 5)

MANAGING MY STRESSORS

My <u>Plans</u> for the Things I Can Control	My <u>Prayers</u> for the Things I Cannot Control

APPENDIX VII
(CHAPTER 5)

CLEAR YOUR HEAD BEFORE BED ACTIVITY

(Complete the phrases below thirty minutes before bedtime nightly.)

Today I am grateful and happy that I accomplished:

_____

_____

_____

Tomorrow I will Prioritize:

_____

_____

_____

Tomorrow I will do these things if I have extra time:

_____

_____

_____

APPENDIX VIII
(CHAPTER 7)

PERSONALIZED STRESS MANAGEMENT PLAN (PSMP)

I will pay attention to my stress levels by noticing my stress symptoms when my body gives me the signal:

_____

_____

_____

_____

I will not ignore my stress signals and symptoms! I will respond to them and implement my relaxation strategies, which are:

_____

_____

_____

_____

After implementing my relaxation strategies, I will assess and identify my stressors. My stressors are:

_____

_____

_____

_____

I will categorize my stressors to create a plan for the things I can control and release the things I cannot control:

_____

_____

_____

_____

I will make time to process and resolve any issues that are causing me to feel unsettled or robs my peace. My resolutions are:

_____

_____

_____

_____

I will prioritize my health by making time to make nutritious meals that make me feel healthy and energized. These meals are:

_____

_____

_____

_____

I will prioritize exercise weekly for at least thirty minutes to improve my body's functioning and produce serotonin naturally. My ideal exercise routine and the best times to exercise are:

_____

_____

_____

_____

I will practice good sleep hygiene that will help me to feel rested and have a balanced mood. My bedtime routine will be:

_____

_____

_____

_____

I will identify the areas of priority in my life (myself, family, work, spirituality, friendships, community, special interests, etc.). How much time will each activity require to ensure that I have the balance I need. My daily and weekly schedule to create balance in my life is as follows: Daily Schedule (meditation, work, meals, exercise, family/social, sleep, etc.):

Weekly Schedule: (meditation, work, meals, exercise, family/social, sleep, etc.):

_____

_____

_____

_____

I will accept God's plan for me to live an abundant and fulfilling life by:

- Participating in the following self-care activities:
- Connecting with the following people who love me and who I love:
- Engaging in the following activities that bring me joy and lots of laughter:

APPENDIX IX

(CHAPTER 9)

TEN BIBLICAL REFERENCES OF GOD'S LOVE FOR YOU

1. **Romans 8:38–39** (NIV) "For I am convinced that neither death nor life, neither angels nor demons, neither the present nor the future, nor any powers, neither height nor depth, nor anything else in all creation, will be able to separate us from the love of God that is in Christ Jesus our Lord."

2. **Ephesians 2:4–5** (NIV) "But because of his great love for us, God, who is rich in mercy, made us alive with Christ even when we were dead in transgressions—it is by grace you have been saved."

3. **1 John 4:9–10** (NIV) "This is how God showed his love among us: He sent his one and only Son into the world that we might live through him. This is love: not that we loved God, but that he loved us and sent his Son as an atoning sacrifice for our sins."

4. **John 3:16** (NIV) "For God so loved the world that he gave his one and only Son, that whoever believes in him shall not perish but have eternal life."

5. **Zephaniah 3:17** (NIV) "The Lord your God is with you, the Mighty Warrior who saves. He will take great delight in you; in his love he will no longer rebuke you, but will rejoice over you with singing."

6. **Psalm 136:26** (NIV) "Give thanks to the God of heaven. His love endures forever."

7. **Jeremiah 31:3** (NIV) "The Lord appeared to us in the past, saying: 'I have loved you with an everlasting love; I have drawn you with unfailing kindness.'"

8. **Titus 3:4-5** (NIV) "But when the kindness and love of God our Savior appeared, he saved us, not because of righteous things we had done, but because of his mercy. He saved us through the washing of rebirth and renewal by the Holy Spirit."

9. **1 John 4:16** (ESV) "So we have come to know and to believe the love that God has for us. God is love, and anyone who abides in love abides in God, and God abides in them."

10. **Psalm 103:8** (NIV) "The Lord is compassionate and gracious, slow to anger, abounding in love."

11. These Bible texts highlight the unconditional love of God for humanity, emphasizing His everlasting and unfailing love, demonstrated through the gift of His Son, Jesus Christ, and the salvation offered through Him. They also emphasize God's compassion, grace, and mercy toward us, underscoring that nothing can separate us from His love.

APPENDIX X
ENDNOTES

CHAPTER 1

1 Selye, H. (1936). A syndrome produced by diverse nocuous agents. Nature, 138(3479), 32.

2 Selye, H. (1950). Stress and the general adaptation syndrome. British Medical Journal, 1(4667), 1383–1392.

3 Selye, H. (1936). A syndrome produced by diverse nocuous agents. Nature, 138(3479), 32.

4 APA Dictionary of Psychology.

5 Yale Medicine Interdisciplinary Stress Center, Fact Sheets, "Chronic Stress," https://www.yalemedicine.org/conditions/stress-disorder

6 Yale Medicine Interdisciplinary Stress Center, Fact Sheets, "Chronic Stress/Overview," https://www.yalemedicine.org/conditions/stress-disorder

7 Rajita Sinha, PhD, Yale Medicine Interdisciplinary Stress Center, Fact Sheets, "Chronic Stress," https://www.yalemedicine.org/conditions/stress-disorder

8 Rajita Sinha, PhD, Yale Medicine Interdisciplinary Stress Center," What other conditions are related to chronic stress?" https://www.yalemedicine.org/conditions/stress-disorder

9 Yale Medicine Interdisciplinary Stress Center, "The Effects of High Stress on the Brain and Body in Adults" https://medicine.yale.edu/stresscenter/reduction/adult_stress_load_infobrief_210643_284_25866_v1_372850_284_46027_v1.pdf

10 K.N. Poornima, N. Karthick, and R. Sitalakshmi, National Library of Medicine," Study of the Effect of Stress on Skeletal Muscle Function in Geriatrics," https://www.ncbi.nlm.nih.gov/pmc/articles/PMC3939594/

CHAPTER 2

11   American Psychological Association. (2020, October). Stress in America 2020: A National Mental Health Crisis. Retrieved from https://www.apa.org/news/press/releases/stress/2020/report-october

12   April issue of Behavioral Neuroscience, published by the American Psychological Association.

13   American Psychological Association, "Chronic Exposure To Stress Hormone Causes Anxious Behavior In Mice," https://www.science-daily.com/releases/2006/04/060417013315.htm

CHAPTER 4

14   Cohen, S., Kamarck, T., Mermelstein, R. (1983). A global measure of perceived stress. Journal of Health and Social Behavior, 24, 385–396.

CHAPTER 5

15   McEwen, B. S., Nasca, C., & Gray, J. D. (2016). Stress effects on neuronal structure: Hippocampus, amygdala, and prefrontal cortex. Nature Neuroscience, 18(10), 1353–1365.

16   Yale Medicine. (n.d.). Adult stress load: How stress affects your health. Retrieved from https://medicine.yale.edu/stresscenter/reduction/adult_stress_load_infobrief_210643_284_25866_v1_372850_284_46027_v1.pdf

17   "Prayer, Attachment to God, and Symptoms of Anxiety-Related Disorders among U.S. Adults," was published in the journal Sociology of Religion.

18   Lyubomirsky, S., Dickerhoof, R., Boehm, J. K., & Sheldon, K. M. (2011). Becoming Happier Takes Both a Will and a Proper Way: An Experimental Longitudinal Intervention to Boost Well-Being., https://www.ncbi.nlm.nih.gov/pmc/articles/PMC4380267/ .

19   Cohn, M. A., Fredrickson, B. L., Brown, S. L., Mikels, J. A., & Conway, A. M. (2009). Happiness Unpacked: Positive Emotions Increase Life Satisfaction by Building Resilience. Emotion (Washington, D.C.), 9(3), 361. https://doi.org/10.1037/a0015952

20   Pressman, S. D., & Cohen, S. (2005). Does positive affect influence health? Psychological Bulletin, 131(6), 925–971.

21 Bethany E Kok 1, Kimberly A Coffey, Michael A Cohn, Lahnna I Catalino, Tanya Vacharkulksemsuk, Sara B Algoe, Mary Brantley, Barbara L Fredrickson (2013), How positive emotions build physical health: perceived positive social connections account for the upward spiral between positive emotions and vagal tone. https://www.researchgate.net/publication/236643284_How_Positive_Emotions_Build_Physical_Health_Perceived_Positive_Social_Connections_Account_for_the_Upward_Spiral_Between_Positive_Emotions_and_Vagal_Tone

22 Fredrickson, B. L., & Branigan, C. (2005). Positive emotions broaden the scope of attention and thought-action repertoires. Cognition and Emotion, 19(3), 313–332.

23 Bethany E Kok 1, Kimberly A Coffey, Michael A Cohn, Lahnna I Catalino, Tanya Vacharkulksemsuk, Sara B Algoe, Mary Brantley, Barbara L Fredrickson (2013), How positive emotions build physical health: perceived positive social connections account for the upward spiral between positive emotions and vagal tone. https://www.researchgate.net/publication/236643284_How_Positive_Emotions_Build_Physical_Health_Perceived_Positive_Social_Connections_Account_for_the_Upward_Spiral_Between_Positive_Emotions_and_Vagal_Tone

24 Harvard T.H., School of Public Health, The Nutrition Source, Stress and Health, Tips to Help Control Stress, Healthy diet, https://www.hsph.harvard.edu/nutritionsource/stress-and-health/#:~:text=A%20balanced%20diet%20can%20support,help%20to%20regulate%20cortisol%20levels

25 Harvard T.H., School of Public Health, The Nutrition Source, Stress and Health, How Chronic Stress Affects Eating Patterns, Healthy diet, https://www.hsph.harvard.edu/nutritionsource/stress-and-health/#:~:text=A%20balanced%20diet%

26 Centers for Disease Control and Prevention. (2016, February 15). Are you getting enough sleep? Retrieved from https://www.cdc.gov/media/releases/2016/p0215-enough-sleep.html

27 Centers for Disease Control and Prevention. (n.d.). How much sleep do I need? Retrieved from https://www.cdc.gov/sleep/about_sleep/how_much_sleep.html

28   Mayo Clinic. (n.d.). Adjustment disorders – Diagnosis and treatment. Retrieved from https://www.mayoclinic.org/diseases-conditions/adjustment-disorders/diagnosis-treatment/drc-20355230

29   Mayo Clinic Family Health Book, 5th Edition.

30   American Psychiatric Association's Diagnostic and Statistical Manual of Mental Disorders, Fifth Edition (DSM-5).

31   Oxford University Press. (n.d.). Biodiversity, n. In Oxford English Dictionary Online. Retrieved from https://www.oed.com/viewdictionaryentry/Entry/110566

32   Berk, L. S., & Tan, S. A. (2009). Laughter and the immune system: A review of the effects of laughter on the immune system and stress levels in healthy adults. The American Journal of the Medical Sciences, 338(2), 148–152.

33   Berk, L. S., & Tan, S. A. (2009). Laughter and the immune system: A review of the effects of laughter on the immune system and stress levels in healthy adults. The American Journal of the Medical Sciences, 338(2), 148–152.

CONTINUE YOUR JOURNEY TO STRESS-LESS LIVING

To complement your reading experience, I invite you to visit my website, abundanceofpeace.com, where you'll find additional resources, articles, and insights to support your journey to stressing less.

WATCH AND LEARN:

For more tips and strategies, subscribe to my YouTube channel, **The Abundant Life Today**. Here, you'll find videos packed with practical advice and techniques to help you achieve a harmonious and balanced life.

ENROLL IN THE COURSE:

Take your stress management journey to the next level by enrolling in my course, **Stress Less: How to Achieve Harmony and Balance in your Life: The R.E.A.L Stress Management Strategy**. This course is designed to provide you with hands-on activities and in-depth strategies to help you experience true harmony and balance in your life.

COURSE HIGHLIGHTS:

- **Interactive modules** filled with practical exercises.
- **Personalized stress management plans.**
- **Supportive community** and expert guidance.

REGISTER NOW!

Don't miss out on this opportunity to transform your life. Register for the course today and take the first step towards a stress-free, harmonious, and balanced life. Visit abundanceofpeace.com to sign up.

STAY CONNECTED:

Follow me on social media and stay updated with the latest tips, courses, and resources:

Website: abundanceofpeace.com

Facebook.com/TheabundantlifeTodaycounseling

Linkedin.com/company/abundance-of-peace-counselling/

Embark on your journey to a stress-less life today with Stress Less: How to Achieve Harmony and Balance in your Life: The R.E.A.L Stress Management Strategy. Your path to peace and balance starts here!